A Fruit-Bearing Spirituality

A Fruit-Bearing Spirituality

Carolyn Reinhart

Winchester, UK
Washington, USA

First published by Circle Books, 2013
Circle Books is an imprint of John Hunt Publishing Ltd., Laurel House, Station Approach,
Alresford, Hants, SO24 9JH, UK
office1@jhpbooks.net
www.johnhuntpublishing.com
www.circle-books.com

For distributor details and how to order please visit the 'Ordering' section on our website.

Text copyright: Carolyn Reinhart 2013

ISBN: 978 1 78099 441 3

A CIP catalogue record for this book is available from the British Library.

Design: Stuart Davies

Printed in the USA by Edwards Brothers Malloy

We operate a distinctive and ethical publishing philosophy in all
areas of our business, from our global network of authors to
production and worldwide distribution.

CONTENTS

Anyone not shocked by Quantum Theory has not understood it.
—Neils Bohr

The day will come when after we have mastered the winds, the waves, the tides and gravity, we shall harness for God the energies of love. Then for the second time in the history of the world, man will have discovered fire.
—Teilhard de Chardin

Foreword

This book is the outcome of decades of spiritual searching and itself the fruit of a pastoral practice rooted in ecological awareness. With painful honesty and a shining integrity Carolyn Reinhart guides us through the steps of her spiritual praxis and discovery, continually encouraging us by the excitement she has experienced and shares. Many will resonate with the obstacles she has overcome – like institutional religion and theology's attempts to downgrade spirituality, or at least to fail to recognise its crucial significance; as well as the obtuse and off-putting nature of much technical jargon associated with theology. The vision of spirituality is here one that can be embraced by many world religious traditions.

Beginning with a simple intuition that an inclusive spirituality that refuses to be privatised is the first pointer: we are then led through an eight-fold path. Highlights of this are the connecting of inner and outer dimensions, (thereby overcoming dualisms), the centrality of praxis and the desire for transformation, a transformation that embraces self and world.

The uniqueness of the journey offered here is not only that Reinhart is immersed in the insights of Quantum physics – through Dana Zohar' work – but that she integrates these with the spiritual path, so that ideas of connectedness, mutuality, and relationships mutually reinforce each other: "we can live our quantum relationships and spirituality together", she asserts meaningfully. She has the humility to listen to the wisdom of many wise guides in the field, whose insights are then integrated into her own pathway. The achievement of the "fruit bearing spirituality" is to indicate to us who strive for justice and liberation, that this struggle can be an integrated part of "revolutionary mysticism" – itself part of a spirituality that continues to evolve.

Mary Grey, University of Winchester, UK
Visiting Professor, St Mary's University College, Twickenham, UK

Preface

This book is different in two ways from most spiritualities. First, it connects any sort of inward journey with an outward movement toward community and justice. Second, it uses quantum physics to undergird the efficaciousness of spirituality. These are not mind games; something really happens to persons as they develop a deeper sense.

This book is the fruit of a study that came out of my own life-long struggle and journey, especially in my Masters and Doctoral studies. Yet it is designed for those beginning or reassessing their spiritual journeys. My hope is that you will want to journey deeply in order to discover more understanding of your own journey and soul searching.

I completed a Masters of Arts degree in Christian Spirituality in 1999 at Heythrop College, University of London. This gave me an excellent grounding in the what of spirituality. Something seemed lacking however, so I completed my Doctorate in Professional Studies with The National Centre for Work Based Learning, Middlesex University, London, UK. My dissertation was "Developing a Spirituality Praxis within a Multidisciplinary Organization". Equally important in my work is that for over 30 years, I lived in lay Christian Communities, which also yielded experiential learning at many levels.

Many persons have helped me along the way. My interest in theology and God's presence was evident even throughout high school. I used to go on retreats, which I loved. Instead of entering the convent as some of my classmates and friends did, I decided to become a nurse so I could join the White Sisters of Africa to work with lepers. Brother Damian wrote a book about his starting a leper colony, which inspired me. Other books, such as Thomas Merton's *No Man Is an Island*, were also important.

After my training as a registered nurse in Ontario, Canada, and working within the field for ten years, I moved to the United

Kingdom, to join Post Green Community in Dorset. During those years, I trained with Frank Lake, a psychiatrist and Founder of the Clinical Theology Association. Several of us in the Community did the Association's two year Pastoral Counselling Course. He then mentored me during the last two years of his life.

Several of us in the community also trained in Spiritual Direction with Reverend Brian Hawker and Reverend Christine Clarke for two years and then with Bishop Graham Chadwick and Gerry Hughes S.J. for several years. This training helped me to grow both in my personal and theoretical understanding of Spiritual Direction or what we preferred to call Spiritual Accompaniment.

In 1984, within the context of Post Green Community I founded Post Green Pastoral Centre, in order to organize formally the existing and on-going ministry we had in pastoral care, counselling and teaching. Our particular interest was to be able to help people to integrate their spiritual and emotional lives, something that many people were crying out for within the UK. We offered counselling, spiritual direction, retreats, conferences, and workshops as well as publishing small booklets on related subjects. We had on-going supervision and training.

Between 1990 and 1996, as a community, we founded Holton Lee, a Centre for Disabled People and caregivers, set on the edge of Poole Harbour. Then I spent four years in Participative Action Research with a group of five other people within the organization. Thank you to my co-researchers who met with me monthly: Tony Heaton, (Director), Jeanne Hinton and Alan Greening (Trustees), Dr Julie Walker (Land Manager) and Jean Greening (Volunteer Counsellor). They were from various denominations or faith beliefs or none. All of the Trustees were supportive as was Post Green Community and *Sir Thomas and Lady Lees* and the Lees family who were also founding members of Holton Lee. It was on their land that both Post Green Community and Holton Lee existed.

At the time, I didn't know how important Holton Lee would be for me. Yet it became central as I framed my research question: How can Holton Lee best establish a Spirituality Praxis? Our attempt, as an organization, was to integrate mutually the Four Aspects, namely, the Arts, Environment, Disability, and Spirituality-Personal Growth. This book grows out of that experience. I do thank my tutors at Heythrop College, in particular, Dr Valerie Lesniak, who gave us the initial grounding and understanding of what the new academic field of spirituality meant. Then I thank the National Centre for Work Based Learning for their dedicated assistance in helping me to deal with what they acknowledged as a very complex and multifaceted Research Project and in particular Prof Derek Portwood who was the founder of the Centre, and my supervisor.

I moved back to Canada in 2005 after some 30 years in the UK. In Muskoka, Ontario, I have found a sense of community in Huntsville especially within the Arts Community and also a home within the surrounding natural environment which continues to nourish and challenge me. I have a continuing passion to share both textually and with photography.

When I mention spirituality in this book, it is not from within the context of any particular faith or religion or belief system. No one denomination or faith has ownership of spirituality. The Spirit is inclusive and not exclusive, which would, in fact, be an antithesis of true spirituality. When I talk about the Divine, the Other, Higher Power, Spirit, God, the Unnameable, Mystery, Love – it is only a matter of language difference or preference. People refer to their own Deity in many different ways. According to Norin ni Riain, Dias is the word that the Irish language uses for God; Dio the Italians, and so on. Father Adrian Smith writes that it is not doctrine which divides us but rather language itself.

So let us blend our words and insights until we understand and keep each other safe. Over the past several years, I have especially appreciated and benefited from The Wisdom University, The Mystery School, Ions, Deepak Chopra, The Shift, Diarmuid

O'Murchu, Brian Swimme, Judy Cannato, Thomas Berry, Cynthia Bourgeault, David Abram, Caroline Myss, Norm Sheely, Jean Houston, and others. They are exploring spirituality, consciousness and awareness-raising and quantum physics at various levels for the sake of our earth home. We are in a global crisis at so many and escalating levels, as we all know. The general intention is to gather together, somehow, with shared intent, to become more healthy, integrated and authentic as individuals and collectively, so that more sound decisions are made within our personal and global lives and home.

I want to thank all the many people who have helped me and accompanied me in my journey over the years: teachers, mentors, friends, and family. All were and are important and too numerous to mention. I would particularly like to thank two specific mentors who were so influential in my life for many years. They are Faith Lees with whom I worked for twenty years and Dr Frank Lake. Most latterly, however, I would like to thank Dr Marge Dennis, who initially laboured for long hours with me in a process of creativity, also my housemate and community friend Geraldine O'Meara. We ran the Pastoral Centre together and then she had to put up with so many years of my study and the accompanying crises and needs. My sisters have supported me through prayer all along; they are Pat, Sandi and Diane. Dr Michael Higgins suggested several years ago over a cup of coffee and discussion about my doctorate that I should make the Doctoral Thesis into a book. I took his suggestion seriously and now eleven years later I have done it. So thank you, Michael.

In addition, there have been many readers whose comments have helped shape and re-shape the various drafts of this book. In particular they are Sharon McNally, Geraldine O'Meara, Sandi Reinhart, and Timothy Staveteig. Jeanne Hinton, a writer, and Debbie Thorpe, a retired publisher, both long-standing friends in the UK were specifically helpful and encouraging from their professional perspectives.

Introduction

Fruits from the Bottom Up

On the South side of England on the English Channel is the Holton Lee Centre, situated on acres of virgin land. I have many fond memories of the lush countryside, especially many of the oak trees with large canopies of leaves that bud, blossom and shade, and of the acorns dropping and finally the leaves falling after displaying their orangish brown colours. These trees were my inspiration and deliverance because they offered such a clear model of the spirituality displayed at this Centre for Disabled People and Carers (or caregivers). Picture nourishment, wisdom, vision, insight and experience moving up from the roots through the trunk and out into the branches. The leaves cause this inner siphoning action as they draw on the inner moisture while sending their juices out into fruit (acorns) and back down to the earth to create more trees.

If one day lightening were to strike one of these trees, then after the storm had passed we could examine the exposed bark, which attempted to protect the tree; phloem, which transports sap from leaves to the rest of the tree; a thin layer of cambium, which is the growth layer; and the sapwood, which is a pipeline for transporting moisture up to the leaves. At the centre is the heartwood, which is dead sapwood. The leaves, whether skinny pine needles or broad oak leaves and branches, would have served the same purpose of converting carbon dioxide, water, and sunlight into sap (a sugar with nutrients). The roots, which often are as large a bundle underground as the tree's branch-and-leaf crown above ground, complete the system by drawing up moisture and using the sap for growth as enlargement and extension.

Trees and Spirituality

A first connection of the tree with spirituality is that both grow from the ground up. A tree places its roots in the soil to draw up only the nutrients needed while ignoring, even resisting things that are not healthy for it. We have already taken in unhealthy things. We need to identify those attitudes and beliefs which are contrary to living and bearing the fruit of good trees.

The parts and functions we see are really a whole thing that works together to grow, blossom and produce. In humans, what is produced is the key to understanding that spirituality. As Jesus says in Matthew 7: "Are grapes gathered from thorns, or figs from thistles? In the same way, every good tree bears good fruit, but every bad tree bears bad fruit." Every religion seems to make a similar affirmation.

A second connection is that both are influenced by their soils or contexts. As I grew in understanding and spiritual expression, I had several major questions about my own context, wondering how to appropriate and truly live out my own new deep learning. Patriarchy, dominance, and power-over people, I learned, were not an authentic or a loving way of living, nor was living in oppression and under that dominance a healthy way of life. I began to see so many places where this way of life was being lived out, and this presented so many challenges to me.

These places were within the Church, my ecumenical lay Christian community, which I had been part of for thirty years and even within the structures of the charity organisation. The suggestion of our tutors was to see things through the lens of our contexts. In the masters, we also studied third world spirituality, women's spirituality, the Church structure and context and the concern for the environment. I could no longer, for the sake of justice and my own integrity, ignore what I saw and experienced. I began to challenge, ask questions and change or leave those unhealthy, inauthentic contexts—which stated one thing and practiced another—because those structures were oppressive.

There are two basic models of systems and how they operate. One is dominant, top-down, power hungry, unjust, not living out right relationships. Even after years of countering sexism, racism, classism, and all the other -isms, these systems are still generated. One model that is promoted in this book – and that fits the metaphor of a tree – is bottom-up, vision sharing, just, and seeks to live in harmony with others. The first type tries to make things grow by pulling on the branches; the second type makes things grow by sharing the soil and its nutrients.

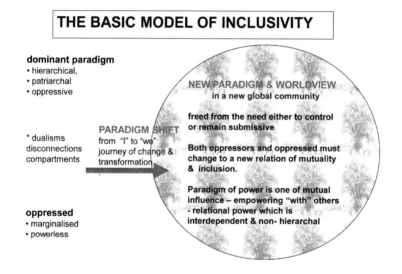

THE BASIC MODEL OF INCLUSIVITY

dominant paradigm
• hierarchical,
• patriarchal
• oppressive

* dualisms
disconnections
compartments

PARADIGM SHIFT
from "I" to "we"
journey of change &
transformation

oppressed
• marginalised
• powerless

NEW PARADIGM & WORLDVIEW
in a new global community

freed from the need either to control
or remain submissive

Both oppressors and oppressed must
change to a new relation of mutuality
& inclusion.

Paradigm of power is one of mutual
influence – empowering "with" others
- relational power which is
interdependent & non- hierarchal

The second model emerged over the years in the actual research process as we continued to be alert to combine theory and practice. We became aware of the various definite stages or phases, which finally totalled eight in number. This second model is splayed out in chapters 1 through 8.

A third connection is that both grow from the inside out. Many persons who study spirituality grow in knowledge and perhaps good feelings. Yet nothing emerges into the world because growth is not obtained or realised. The reason is that

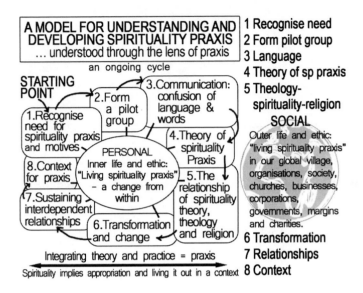

A MODEL FOR UNDERSTANDING AND DEVELOPING SPIRITUALITY PRAXIS
... understood through the lens of praxis

an ongoing cycle

STARTING POINT

2.Form a pilot group

3.Communication: confusion of language & words

1.Recognise need for spirituality praxis and motives

PERSONAL
Inner life and ethic: "Living spirituality praxis" – a change from within

4.Theory of spirituality Praxis

8.Context for praxis

5.The relationship of spirituality theory, theology and religion

7.Sustaining interdependent relationships

6.Transformation and change

Integrating theory and practice = praxis

Spirituality implies appropriation and living it out in a context

1 Recognise need
2 Form pilot group
3 Language
4 Theory of sp praxis
5 Theology-spirituality-religion
SOCIAL
Outer life and ethic: "living spirituality praxis" in our global village, organisations, society, churches, businesses, corporations, governments, margins and charities.
6 Transformation
7 Relationships
8 Context

they have approached spirituality as though it is a theory. It has theoretical components, but it also is a practice.

We need to combine theory and practice into a *praxis*, which is theory-informing practice and practice-informing theory. With such a dynamic flow back and forth, we are on a journey of growth, change, and hopefully transformation.

Just as a tree has a moisture up-sap down cycle, so our transformation is a circular process. In the present moment when we encounter a problem or question we can then consider options and reflect on the best decision or way forward. Then we act on that decision and experience what happens. Later, once we experience the fruit of our decision, we can spend time reflecting on what happened and consider whether the decision was the most helpful or expedient for us.

This concept of cycles is important. Life is not lived on a straight line. Our journey is not simply a series of rational decisions moving from A to B, but rather a series of experiences where we can choose our response and way forward.

The fruit and insights of such action-reflection-revised action changed my life at a deep level. It was transformative only in as much as I chose to take on board and live out that which I was learning. I still find the material and what I learned from it – and am still learning – so exciting and revealing.

Praxis

SPIRITUALITY PRAXIS

THEORY ←——→ PRACTICE

INFORM EACH OTHER RESULTING IN
CHANGE AND TRANSFORMATION

One of the first and key understandings for me in considering the research question and methodology design was to understand praxis. That is if you combine theory and practice you get *praxis*, which is theory-informing practice and practice-informing theory. That is true in the field of spirituality as in any field. I realized that we could learn a new, relevant and authentic theory of spirituality, which then would inform our living, and in turn our living experience would shape and inform our theory about spirituality.

To consider spiritual praxis, we need to change metaphors to our lives as journeys. As Aristotle once said, the difference between plants and animals is that animals can move around while plants are, well, planted.

Our lives are not static and stationary. There is constant change. As was stated above we are on a journey of growth, change and hopefully transformation, growing into who we were created to be.

The two models, which are shared in subsequent chapters

here, might look simple yet the arrow is critical because it represents the journey of transformation!

Both oppressors and oppressed must change. A paradigm shift– along with significant transformation at personal, group, family, organizational, national, and world levels – must occur, and we can see more clearly without the constraints of our previous programming, experiences, projections and collusions. We are set free to see in a new way with new eyes and hearts and then be able to have more considered responses and make more healthy decisions.

The journey of change on which we embark when we begin to become more aware and conscious of life in and around us, is really a journey of transformation at every level of our beings and continues for the rest of our lives. It isn't easy or automatic and we have to decide and choose what we want and how committed we will be. The more we learn, the more intense the journey is, and we seem to get more deeply involved in life, in our wider social contexts rather than thinking as some people do, that spirituality is very personal only. Instead, it really affects the whole of our lives: our bodies, minds and spirits; how we spend our time, money, and resources; our friendships and relationships; our politics, sexuality, energy, family and so on. There is not one aspect of our lives that is untouched.

Living praxis required me to write from both my head (authentic academically) and heart. This was very challenging – requiring personal experience, integration and a search to find words and text to match or express that reality – language! It was yet another aspect of my journey that I felt I could "not" do and so for the past nine years I continued to study and "experience" more.

We Are All One

Some dimensions of spirituality are very broad. Spirituality is both personal and social, and has to do with the uniqueness of our being. It is non-material and is also a process in which we follow our own path, on our own journey. It gives us life. It is something a reflective person knows and is aware of in varying degrees. It is different from humanitarianism. Our spirituality informs and forms all aspects of our lives.

We have not mentioned, however, the various forms of spirituality and different types of practices, such as eco-feminism, yoga, sexuality (for example, Kama Sutra), Buddhism, quantum physics, psychology, and various denominations or faiths. Yet, we are all still one, joined together in a web of relationships, sharing our earth home and cosmos.

Even in this twenty-first century, we are becoming increasingly more numbed and spiritually silent. Perhaps we are afraid of our spirituality and the surrounding confusion that happens when we think church, religion or theology is synonymous with it. Perhaps we are afraid of the implications of a cost or responsibility to be authentic and to love.

If we are not conscious and aware of our spiritual life as people, then we tend as a result to be poor lovers. Conversely, if we constantly develop our spiritual life, as we would tend and nurture a garden, then we will grow in what Love is. We can't be a spiritual person without being a lover.

"We are all one" means that we are interconnected, that the choices you make have an impact or implication for me; my choices have consequences for you. This also means that life for the oppressed cannot improve until both oppressor and the oppressed are changed. This change comes through wisdom and living (praxis), not through thinking and rationalizing alone (theory) and not through routines and refinements (practice).

Take a look at the other outcome. When we encounter what we often call blocks, brick walls, dark places, or no-go areas, we may want to stop, give up or run away. Often then, we do run away into alcohol, drugs, food, sex or other forms of avoidance to calm our shattered nerves and growing fears. This can be especially the case as we experience our inability to weather these storms or difficulties when we didn't know how to grow and to find light instead of darkness. We may feel overwhelmed, sinking or even drowning. We may seek respite in whatever way we can or have learned how to do. We affect others and ourselves with whatever choice we make and so we alter the journeys of others. Our lives are complex, compounded – and intertwined. We are all one, living in a web of relationships.

Our feelings, thoughts, beliefs and experience may make us think it is a viscous circle with no way out and we feel powerless. However paradoxically, it is at these times of darkness, confusion, despair and fear that there can be deeper growth, change and transformation.

Our lives are journeys which we live alone and also share with others. Our spirituality evolves as we choose our responses to what is happening in us and around us each moment. It comes from inside us and is evolving constantly as we interact with our world around us. We are in a process of living life – a process that is not me or you, but forms and informs and makes us.

A central aspect of being spiritual is to shift from thinking *I* to living *we*.

God-Talk

The language that we use about God can be difficult for each other. It is important to realise this in all discussions and consideration about what words we can use. Or, perhaps there are no words. More than a few have discussed the difficulty and inadequacy of language, especially spiritual language. Some of us carry baggage from our childhood about words used for God. Some people now prefer to use the words such as Higher Power, Energy, Life, I Am, Divine Mystery.

The reality is that no one religion, faith or belief system has a licence or ownership of spirituality – we are all one, sharing together in our web of life, ideally, mutually, reciprocally and with inter-dependence. It is a reality and experience which we live – a Living Reality or Presence and Energy within and around us, whether we recognise it individually or collectively or not. That is we can be living it either authentically or in an unhealthy way.

Remember, we can tell if we are living with the Spirit by the fruits of our lives and how we relate to others. Descriptions such as love, kindness, care, inclusiveness, in patience and mutual relationship should be used by those who observe our lives.

Growing in Love, not Fear

With a wide range for God-talk language, and with the ability to ascertain paths by their fruits, we need to explain another important aspect of spirituality. Spirituality is not a religion or a belief system or a reasoning system like theology. To be spiritual is not to join a cult or go to worship on Sundays. Those fearful of these things need not worry. You will not be asked to follow some self-styled guru or practitioner.

In fact, we need to grow into love and let go of fear – that is transformation (King, Zohar, Myss, Hughes). Whether we know it or not, we are on our spiritual journey with others and with the Mystery, Love or Higher Power. Our search for meaning, truth, reality, integrity, authenticity and love continues throughout our life's journey. We never arrive as such, but we are continually searching in many places and in many ways. We search with our minds, hearts and bodies. We search alone and with others.

Many opinions, points of view, theories, theologies, books and spiritualities are available. For example, according to Cashmore and Puls, fifty-two types of spirituality are readily available – along with individuals and groups offering us help on the way to one or another of them. Some are deemed authentic and some are not. There is also a proliferation of books and websites. Some books are centuries old, written by saints and mystics and containing a wealth of wisdom and experience.

Our journeys are both into our inner selves along with a realization of our outer selves and lives we live in the world context around us – with all that is happening and all the realities presented. We are not alone; we do not live on an island. We live in a context, both locally and globally.

In our letting go of our fearfully and tightly held perspectives and beliefs something new happens in our cycle of transformation; we can begin to integrate our experiences and life-styles with growing awareness, (that is consciousness, alertness, wakefulness, attentiveness, consciousness according to the thesaurus).

In letting go we begin to experience mystery and wisdom, not just our thinking that is often rigid, fearful, and full of logic and certainty. We find we aren't afraid of imagination and our feelings, even if it all seems confusing and not the same as we are used to. We probably won't even feel we have any answers but we can live in peace with all the questions, as we rest more on intuition and inspiration in our cycle of transformation and our leap of faith or quantum leap and paradigm shift.

Spirituality and Quantum Physics

Physics and spirituality need to take the next step together for the wisdom of our separate disciplines is incomplete on its own – an interconnection and interconnectedness.

Spirituality is uniquely oriented toward an emerging global society that fosters a collaborative desire for peace in neighbourhoods and nations. (Miriam Therese Winters)

As Zohar writes, to have a successful worldview we must draw personal, social and spiritual into one coherent whole. We must therefore be in touch with our own experiences and deepest intuitions to have our knowledge of the world and ourselves. Quantum physics gives a physical basis to a more holistic, less fragmented way of looking at ourselves, realising that the whole world of creation shares a physics with everything else in the universe: with the human body, all other living creatures, the coherent ground state, matter and relationships and the quantum vacuum itself. This vacuum is not empty but is the basic, fundamental underlying reality of which everything in this universe, including ourselves, is an expression. It is like a bubbling soup or is a theory of everything. Quantum field theory proposes the link between the physics of human consciousness and the physics of the quantum vacuum. (Zohar)

King, a UK professor and internationally known scholar on spirituality, writes that

> Spirituality can be linked to all human experiences, but it has a particularly close connection with the imagination, with human creativity and resourcefulness, with relationships – whether with ourselves, with others, or with a transcendent reality, named or unnamed, but often called the Divine, God or Spirit. Spirituality can also be connected with a sense of celebration and joy, with adoration and surrender, with struggle and suffering – the global dimensions of this quest, which are rooted in the earth and connected to the diversity of peoples, cultures, and faiths around the world.

She explains that this has a transformative quality as lived experience, linked to our bodies, nature and our relationship with others and society. This experience seeks the fullness of life, of justice and peace and integrating body, mind and soul, living in a world that has become more globally interdependent, while still so painfully torn apart.

She notes that, "spirituality is no longer a luxury of life ... but appears as an absolute imperative for human sanity and survival. Spirituality is essential to all human flourishing, wherever we live, whether in religious or secular surroundings."

King points out that the hallmarks of a mature spirituality are to take seriously integrity, wisdom and transcendence. It cannot remain the privilege of a few – the religious and educated elite – but needs to permeate social life at all levels. It cannot just be a quest for inner peace but must provide energy and input to the global problems of poverty, homelessness, and human rights violations.

She writes in her recent book, *The Search for Spirituality – Our Global Quest for a Spiritual Life* (2008) that

> A global awakening has to occur on a much larger scale than exists at present. For this, we need education that is more spiritual at all levels. Only then can we achieve wide spiritual literacy, a literacy that goes far beyond learning to read and write, beyond the acquisition of professional training and skills. It also goes beyond emotional and ethical literacy to a much deeper dimension of insight and wisdom that grows from the heart and fosters love and compassion. These are the deepest energy resources humans possess, and the global community is still far from drawing on the transformative power of these resources in all situations of need. To explore the different forms of spirituality in the contemporary world, whether secular, humanistic, scientific, or artistic, and explore their joint potential to enhance and augment the fullness of life, can give ground for new hope. We need ideas to think and work with, to inspire and transform us. To develop consciously spiritual literacy by providing spiritual education and fostering spiritual awakening is one such idea. (King 1992, 2008)

My book is dedicated to offering "more spiritual education" toward the "deeper dimension of insight and wisdom."

A Simple Model Introduced

The research behind this book elicited two models. I explain the first here so it can be understood and applied as we progress in the sharing of the process of learning. The second model is expressed in Chapter 1.

The model of inclusivity emerged into consciousness during a time of quiet reflection and prayer. I believe that it is simple and can be used within any circumstance, situation or context. On the left side are two arrows in opposition. One comes from the top down and represents power over and dominance. The other, from the bottom up represents those who live under such dominance: the victimized, oppressed and those existing under the thumb of power.

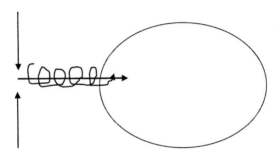

The victimized cannot be released from their victimization until the victimizers are stopped. Yet notice that the victimizers cannot stop their victimization until the victims are released.

From the tension point of these two opposing arrows, a third arrow moves toward the right-hand direction. Here victimizers and the victimized can circle around this arrow as they explore distinctly opposing concepts, such as male-female, gay-straight, white-black, first world-third world. Gradually, people and situations are changed and transformed until we can all live in a relationship of mutuality and equal power–represented by the large oval sphere.

This Basic Model of Inclusivity can be used within marriage

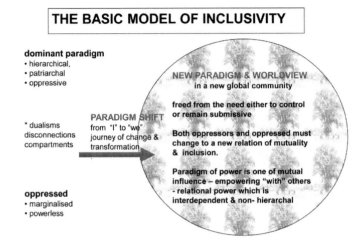

THE BASIC MODEL OF INCLUSIVITY

dominant paradigm
• hierarchical,
• patriarchal
• oppressive

* dualisms
disconnections
compartments

PARADIGM SHIFT
from "I" to "we"
journey of change &
transformation

NEW PARADIGM & WORLDVIEW
in a new global community

freed from the need either to control
or remain submissive

Both oppressors and oppressed must
change to a new relation of mutuality
& inclusion.

Paradigm of power is one of mutual
influence – empowering "with" others
- relational power which is
interdependent & non- hierarchal

oppressed
• marginalised
• powerless

relationships, families, businesses, churches, schools, that is, any structure or relationship. We can use it as a heuristic device to sketch out oppositional problems as well as ways forward. Former combatants can more easily see what is going on, how the context in which we are living is structured, and whether we are being oppressed or seeking more power.

Part One

Embarking on the Journey

Chapter 1

Eight Steps to an Inner Spiritual Praxis

An inner spiritual praxis begins when someone recognises a need. The Introduction closed by describing a simple model of opposition moving toward reconciliation and concord. This insight led us to develop a model with eight stages or steps. At the heart is spirituality praxis lived out in our life, ethic, and context. Note I speak here about a lived-out ethic, not some imposed practice. The goal of our research process was to integrate the founding theology to the practice of *The Now*, for the sake of *The Tomorrow*. Specifically, we had identified four founding aspects at Holton Lee: the arts, disability, the environment, and spirituality. We knew we were researching not only for ourselves but also for transnational global needs and ethics as part of a wider context for praxis.

We encountered another need – namely, a persistent conflict between theology and spirituality; this had to be resolved if we were to achieve our goal not to live a compartmentalised life. Some might think this odd. After all, isn't spirituality a private matter in a particular understanding of God, just as is faith?

We rejected such a privatised spirituality as one that does not seek justice. Why is this important? Because a private spirituality can exist only by ignoring tensions between inner and outer ethics. Thus, we became increasingly more aware of the need to move from the Dominant Mechanistic Paradigm to the Inclusive and Spiritual Paradigm, as individuals and as an organisation. By Dominant Mechanistic, I mean the corporate or military model of top-down, command and control, levers and springs, and the like.

The second model – the Model for Understanding and Developing Spirituality Praxis – also emerged and was refined as we asked what next needed to be dealt with in order to deepen our understanding on our journey, that is as we continued to link emerging theory and practice which resulted in praxis. Eight specific phases emerged, were defined and named and are illustrated below.

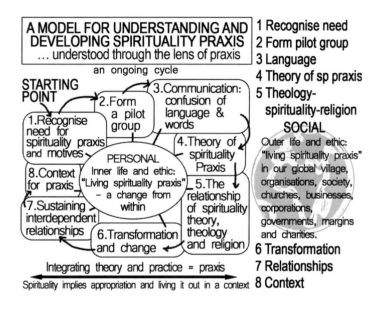

A MODEL FOR UNDERSTANDING AND DEVELOPING SPIRITUALITY PRAXIS
... understood through the lens of praxis

an ongoing cycle

STARTING POINT

1.Recognise need for spirituality praxis and motives

2.Form a pilot group

3.Communication: confusion of language & words

PERSONAL
Inner life and ethic: "Living spirituality praxis" – a change from within

4.Theory of spirituality Praxis

5.The relationship of spirituality theory, theology and religion

6.Transformation and change

7.Sustaining interdependent relationships

8.Context for praxis

Integrating theory and practice = praxis

Spirituality implies appropriation and living it out in a context

1 Recognise need
2 Form pilot group
3 Language
4 Theory of sp praxis
5 Theology-spirituality-religion
SOCIAL
Outer life and ethic: "living spirituality praxis" in our global village, organisations, society, churches, businesses, corporations, governments, margins and charities.
6 Transformation
7 Relationships
8 Context

This model of facilitation describes the theory and our experience of what is involved to enable a widening global view and transformational process to help us to live and appropriate true spirituality. I will use the model to focus our findings with its eight phases forming the sections of this chapter and then include the social consideration.

Our work on this eight-step process also prompts a need. More educators, spiritual guides or spiritual directors are needed so that we do not simply live out our ego by only changing at a superficial level. We need to change deeply in order to be able to live in the reality that we are all connected, as part of each other (as quantum physics indicates, within our relationships, organisations and world).

Spirituality praxis, as experience, is at the heart of the research model and cycle because what is seen and known is from where one stands. Therefore, spirituality is understood through the lens of praxis – not theory, formulas, or techniques only – but from what is experienced, affective, heartfelt, lived and learned deeply. Thus praxis is at the hub of the wheel; the spokes link the centre to all the other aspects or phases. *Inner and outer praxis* are connected through integrating sound theory and good practice. The context, environment, and atmosphere created within an ethos of love and care is important so that there can be inner and outer integration, conducive to authentic praxis, which determines whether we can walk the talk or not. The model can be understood as an on-going cycle since life is on-going and we never stop learning.

Implementing the model should seem natural. This model emerged and was assembled as comprehensive "living theory". I have numbered them but all the phases overlap and are part of each other.

Phase One: Recognise the Need and Motives for Developing Spirituality

What do you want to accomplish in your work place or organization? Perhaps you want to add a spirituality dimension in order to become current with a trend that has been developing prolifically over the past ten years or more. For instance, the main motive could be to help employees or volunteers feel more worthwhile or content so that they can be more productive.

Phase Two: Form a Pilot Group

The research group process requires that each person be committed to the research and development process. The need for a research process can start with an individual and end with a group. Because there is great need for collaborative relationships, great skill is also needed. (Coghlan and Brannick, 2001)

Critten suggests that instead of getting in outside consultants, an organisation should start where the energy is, with what he terms a *pilot group,* which consists of a few individuals who are committed, thinking beyond the present moment and able to surface and codify knowledge that has grown out of the group. (Critten, 1998)

Phase Three: Clear Up Confusing Communication

Understanding the words we each used to talk about spirituality led to highlighting it as a phase of the emerging model. Words were limited and limiting as we attempted to share our knowing, believing, experiences and emerging understanding, particularly because spirituality refers to the more subtle dimensions of awareness. Dorothee Soelle adds that our dominant culture restricts our language and capacity for each, and that theological language has been stripped of narrative qualities so expresses itself in a void of consciousness, empty of emotion and insensitive to human experience and therefore ghost-like.

She suggests, for example, that now we need to seek non-authoritarian, non-patriarchal language to describe a God

whose attributes are not those of distance, power, and domination? We need a language that takes our emotions seriously because when experiences of God break through our existing limitations of human comprehension it is difficult to communicate these experiences; in fact... it is impossible to speak of what lies beyond the capabilities of speech – yet we feel compelled to speak of it. Then the language we use may be paradoxical or may lead to silence. In our century, we no longer have a language to describe our experience as we did in the fourteenth century. (Soelle, 1984: 80-90)

The very name of God, used to describe the un-nameable

Ultimate Reality, has passed. For many people, God conjures up images of a super-human person. Church language still implies someone "up there". According to Adrian Smith, the crisis of faith today is not a doctrinal one, but a language one. Faith is not an intellectual assent to a list of doctrines, but a whole framework of beliefs that give meaning to us. It needs to be presented in a language that is meaningful in the context of people's present day knowledge of spirituality, anthropology, physics and cosmology. We need a language that can express the expanded paradigm of today's knowledge which quantum physics and the cosmological picture science is giving us. Science and religion are both pursuing the truth along adjacent paths; there can be no contradiction. (Smith, 2002:115-119).

Bishop Richard Holloway states that language and the role of speech as well as organisational and ethical systems – these are all part of consideration of spirituality. (Holloway, 1992)

Phase Four: Combine Understanding and Action

SPIRITUALITY PRAXIS

THEORY ←——→ PRACTICE

**INFORM EACH OTHER RESULTING IN
CHANGE AND TRANSFORMATION**

Praxis was a difficult concept to understand and apply. The word itself presented misunderstanding and difficulty at the outset because it seemed a trendy but not understandable word, which some thought would only add confusion to those involved and to readers. They suggested instead using the word practice, which actually has a different meaning and therefore can't be inter-changed. Praxis is defined as: reflexive practice informed by theory. (Zuber-Skerritt, 1994:11)

Praxis means understanding how theory and practice combine into informed action within a context. At Holton Lee, that included an integration of the four aspects; namely, the arts, environment, disability, and spirituality-personal growth.

Praxis is more than practice because praxis means "theory informing practice," as interplay between theory and practice. Therefore it is important to understand what it means. There are two uses and interpretations of the word, one from a secular point of view and the other from a spiritual perspective.

Theory and understanding of *secular praxis* recognises that praxis neither occurs in a vacuum nor results from some kind of thoughtless behaviours that existed separately from theory, behaviours to which theory could simply be applied because they have theory embedded within them. In our research process, we found ourselves moving from ignorance and habit, as theory began to inform our practice and it then transformed the ways in which our practice was experienced and understood overall within the organization.

Spirituality praxis also includes both being and doing-practice. As reflected in our research data, it is not just arbitrary doing or practice where anything goes, but the spirituality element to it involves consideration for power, emancipator and libratory transformation, addressing the cultural concerns of our day as well as helping us to know how to live the good life. In the here and now of our praxis, we can begin our knowledge and formulate our critique and interpretation, and so provide norms for human knowledge, activity and transformation. Critical theory insists on continual critiquing of praxis to guard against systemic distortion and false ideologies, which reveal distortions of interest, power, and knowledge.

Phase Five: Join the Emotional and Intellectual

Orthopraxis ("right praxis") is embodied and lived with the whole person – head, heart, hands and feet, overcoming dichotomies and dualisms, experiencing the something more which is not grasped by objective knowledge and which moves out towards the world of others and God. Love for God and neighbour is not separate but fleshed out in daily life along with responsibility for the social sphere as well.

We lived in the gap and on the bridge between spirituality and theology, and found reconciliation through a loving knowledge that transcended reasoning and thinking. It was a loving power that is a compound of wisdom and love, which can flow out on the surrounding world. Spirituality has been and is a religious phenomenon as we live as being-in-love, which is the core of authentic religion. Awareness also permeated our research as a scientific enterprise. Our resultant concrete loving conduct attempted to meet needs and problems by addressing and trying to eliminate the causes within systems so that practice is not shallow. The fruit of combining practice and theory is that there doesn't need to be a separation between the emotional and intellectual. Understanding and living it have been embodied in people in a context that requires socio-political approaches. By exploring together how to live it out without having to separate out religion, theology and spirituality – kept us from further compartmentalizing them. In fact, quite the opposite was achieved by trying to integrate them – it prevented further dichotomy, dualism and separation.

Theologian Sandra Schneiders (1999) offers a brief description of the difference between religion, spirituality, and theology. *Religion* is both a formal practice of a faith built around a modern code, official form of worship and set of scriptures and a cultural system for dealing with ultimate reality, that which transcends individual or social entity, realizing that religious tradition shapes us.

Theology is an intellectual – predominantly analytical, logical, and deductive – separation from concrete human experience and often is said to be "faith seeking understanding" or an on-going intellectual attempt of the church to understand the faith that we live. Recent theological study, however, includes experiences rather than abstract ideas. It recognises a split between religion and spirituality and in fact, admits that mainline religion has failed to address the needs and desires of the seeking community. Possibilities outside the traditional church are exploding and there is a desperate need for enlightened guidance.

Spirituality is an area of study in its own right and not subordinate to theology. Spirituality is interdisciplinary in its concern for spiritual dimensions to life. It examines dimensions of human existence from a variety of standpoints.

Spirituality is not to be confused, as many people do, with spiritualist or spiritualism or psychic, even though they are both non-material experiences.

Spirituality does not lead to dichotomies, splits or dualisms, e.g. rational vs. intuitive, head vs. heart, body vs. Spirit or male vs. female. Spirituality is not given to you all at once, like a jacket you can buy or put on, but rather is a life long journey involving choices at our various challenges, crossroads and aspects of life.

Some call it indefinable, but that is overstatement: different methods applied to different subjects simply yield different conclusions. When persons from fundamentalism to New Age are the investigators or the subjects of study, such a wide range seems reasonable.

Phase Six: Stop Objectifying and Consuming

In order to love unconditionally, we first need to know God's peace at the centre of our own being. This way, space and freedom replace fear and anger. Only then can we look outward to helping others. This type of renewal and change requires us to break down our own barriers. (Lees, 1982)

Psycho-spiritual integration requires us to move from the hierarchical and dualistic perspectives – not along a linear path – but rather a circular spiral path – leaving maps behind as we turn our hearts in the direction of love. Changing the world means changing ourselves in a journey where each step taken toward the Divine is also taken with the fullest human development. An inter-dependence exists between the spiritual, psychological and physical dimensions of our lives. These aspects grow in tandem. An integrated approach includes body, mind and spirit, and a change of consciousness not mere re-alignment. Only then are we more able to live a holistic spirituality. (Ruumet, 1997)

An adaptation from *Radical Grace: Daily Meditations* (p. 8, day 6; *cac@cacradicalgrace.org*) puts this another way:

If we are to see as God sees, we must first become mirrors of what is, what is right in front of us. We must become a no-thing so that we can receive some-thing else as it is. Transformation of consciousness is this: We must be liberated from ourselves as the reference point for reality, stating our preferences moment by moment and making mental commentaries on every event – up or down. It really does not matter whether we like it or not – it just is. A spiritually transformed person stops looking at reality as an object, or even God as an object for my consumption. God becomes the co-seer with us, not the seen. Can you imagine that?

We really need to be saved from the tyranny of our own judgments, opinions and feelings about everything, the undisciplined squads of emotions that T. S. Eliot criticizes in his poetry. Our ego chooses to objectify everybody and everything else in the world–including God. God is never an object but always the one who sees with us. As Meister Eckhart put it, "The eyes with which we look back at God are the very same eyes with which

God first looked at us." That rearranges everything rather nicely.

Phase Seven: Start Relating to Show Love in Reality

In the research data, relationship was emphasised as fundamental to spirituality praxis. Quantum science supports this awareness. We are physically interwoven and are stitches of the same fabric. Thus, we live in interrelationship and connection throughout the whole of our personal and societal lives and so are both affected by our contexts and affect them; there is a connection between the large and small. (Zohar, 1991)

Johnson tells us that we can form relationships in society through revitalising spiritual energy. This can empower a transformative praxis toward a fulfilling future for all. Those who are oppressed can be empowered with a sense of human dignity and self-hood. They are able to live in free and caring relationships in mature spirituality, thus fostering connectedness and solidarity because their self-respect has been enhanced. In this way, we can establish a wise order of relationship in the world. (Johnson, 1998) Lees believes that we need the strength of relationships that show love in reality. Then we can rely more on the words we speak to each other. (Lees, 1982)

Phase Eight: Expand Your Context for Spirituality Praxis

Our research process underscored the importance of maintaining a healthy environment for spirituality praxis. This requires having an appropriate organizational infrastructure and policies. In order to have these, an organization needs to understand community, organization, corporation, management and leadership motives, shared intent, monitor its ethos and move from a dominant to an inclusive spiritual paradigm.

Our process found confirmation in Sheldrake, Soelle, and Schneiders, who have also emphasized the importance of considering context within the field of spirituality. The implications are plain: we need to be in conversation with the social sciences. This socio-political approach is particularly noticeable in liberationist, feminist, and justice-focused approaches to spirituality – and rightly so.

Spirituality praxis, then, emphasizes the social aspect, ethic and life in order to consider the ways in which our inner and outer lives are connected. We know, of course, that inner and outer knowing or change cannot be separated; spiritual praxis requires a journey at both individual and social levels. This reflective work requires us to come to terms with our shadow (our so-called dark side) and learn to accept what is within. (Lorimer, 1998) Healing needs to take place first at inner and outer, personal and transpersonal, individual and collective, social and spiritual, private and planetary levels so we can live in mutuality. Then we can change from adapting ourselves to oppressive social systems and instead live with connection, compassion, community, and co-operation. (Greenspan, 1993)

It is often easier to say what spirituality is not than to try to describe what it is. It certainly is not a set of codes, formula, theory, or church. More people now realize that

* Spirituality includes the whole of their lives,
* Spirituality is present at personal, group, social, and global levels, and that
* Everything is connected, meaning that everything is included in our search.

Chapter 2

Even the Oppressed Need to Change

A key to becoming more aware of our spirituality and to allow it to bear fruit is embracing our inner life socially. That is our personal and social life and journeys are interconnected.

Embracing Our Inner Life Socially

To summarize the central ideas in the journey of change:

1. Change and what is involved
2. Inclusiveness
3. Becoming aware of where we are oppressors or oppressed
4. Realising that both have to change
5. That learning is bottom-up
6. That there is a Paradigm Shift
7. The Model of Inclusivity is important
8. There is no quick-fix

Spirituality is never just one thing, but rather is a series of contradictions. Picture your spirituality as a line into the future. This line represents the thrust or vision of how we want to live ultimately and it includes cycles within cycles on the pathway of our journey to change and transformation.

Spirituality is not exclusive to any one religion, faith, or belief system; nor is love, whether love for ourselves, others, our earth home, or the Divine. Eight world religious traditions can be identified: Judaism, Christianity, Islam, Hinduism, Buddhism, Taoism, Confucianism, and Native American traditions. Yet none of these traditions can claim complete ownership of spirituality.

We all have accompanying responsibilities to love and grow in love. Reflecting on what persons cited in this chapter have stated as to what spirituality means to them, it seems obvious that their spirituality is seen through the lens of their own lives, environment, experience and context as it is with everyone.

Spirituality is not a theory imposed from the top down, but rather is something we experience, feel and know. It grows in us as a tree grows from the bottom up. Spirituality is personal and also social. As many have pointed out, spirituality involves oneself, others, our shared earth home and the Divine.

"Perhaps without even being fully aware of it, religious leaders and their followers through the ages have defined religion largely in terms of love ... both teach and assume the priority of love in religious practice." The Dali Lama states, "All the major religions of the world have similar ideals of Love, the same goal of benefiting humanity through spiritual practice, and the same effect of making their followers into better human beings. Its meaning cannot be captured within the limitations of language, but can more accurately be measured in action, in good will, kindness, forgiveness, compassion toward others and toward all humanity, all of creation. Agape Love is unconditional and altruistic." (Templeton 1999, 2)

As we become more conscious and aware, we recognise that often things in our lives are not as they should or ought to be. Some people are dominant and oppressive in various ways while others are submissive and oppressed, living like victims. When we do not live as equals with even voices and choices, then the result is strife, confusion, power struggles, opposition, anger, arguments and failing relationships. We find that we cannot live and love the way we would prefer and profess to be able to do. We seem to be unable to be who we are or want to be. Our prejudices, biases, old wounds, previous programming and fears – most often hidden – keep us bound in ignorance.

How then can we develop a spirituality in a world of contradictions? The word *praxis*, discussed earlier, simply means that theory informs our practice and that our practice informs our theory. Therefore it isn't just "any" practice or theory but a more understood and developed, relevant, enabling and empowering one which is especially important in a world where many people are living as oppressed/victimized or are dominant oppressors, even unconsciously.

Change occurs as we become aware of when we are oppressors or when we are oppressed. It is simple, really. We recognise that both the oppressors and the oppressed need to change in order to be able to live in a mutuality and inter-relationship, rather than in a dependent relationship. We can then all live with respect, in an inclusive way in a circle or community of mutuality and love.

Paradigm Shift and Appropriation

Developing these diagrams to be able to use and depict what we were learning at both textual and visual-conceptual levels proved to be important. It enabled us more easily to be able to explain in a simpler, more graphic way, what was happening and how our learning and understanding was happening. This was especially true using PowerPoint presentations.

Living spirituality basically means a paradigm shift in our understanding of how to live out our lives. It is not a dogma, but a living theory of transformation through consciousness raising. A paradigm shift means changing from one worldview to a different one. Often we have lived with our current way of life for quite some time. It seems natural and persuasive; this worldview gets confirmed many times each day.

Suppose that we were living in the industrial era. We might believe that machines are making our lives better, even though the factories drew many people from rural areas into cities causing overcrowding and many workers had health problems. Children were trained to operate equipment and, without education, had little way of moving up or out to some other life. Our worldview, however, would help us confirm that machines are labour-saving devices.

Now, let us shift to the technological age. We might believe that technology is making our lives better, even though many workers in third world countries are exploited to manufacture our laptops or writing tablets. Toxic metals may be released into the environment as we exchange new computers for old ones every two or three years Information workers are on duty twenty-four hours a day, seven days a week. Our worldview, however, helps us confirm that technology offers us more interactive connections with others.

A *paradigm shift* means a radical change in somebody's basic concepts, theories, and assumptions about something or an approach to something. For example, one of the major changes in general consciousness occurred when we changed from viewing the world as flat to viewing the world as round.

Being inclusive is essential for understanding and developing spirituality praxis. The understanding is that both the oppressors and the oppressed need to change in order for a new way of living to be possible within a new paradigm. What and how do I need to change and shift as one who is oppressed or as a person who is an oppressor on my journey of growth?

THE BASIC MODEL OF INCLUSIVITY

dominant paradigm
• hierarchical,
• patriarchal
• oppressive

* dualisms
disconnections
compartments

PARADIGM SHIFT
from "I" to "we"
journey of change &
transformation

oppressed
• marginalised
• powerless

NEW PARADIGM & WORLDVIEW
in a new global community

freed from the need either to control or remain submissive

Both oppressors and oppressed must change to a new relation of mutuality & inclusion.

Paradigm of power is one of mutual influence – empowering "with" others - relational power which is interdependent & non- hierarchal

The diagram which has already been explained is depicted here as a visual reminder. It also develops the understanding of the basic model more fully, with more explanation and description.

The emergence of these models in our work at Holton Lee took a long time to become visible and take shape. It was like being in labour, to be able to give birth to images that were being formed inside. Then when they emerged onto paper, they could be shared with others, expanded, or even changed in many ways as people suggested. We could own them together then as our models (or paradigms) and use them together with others to explain what we were learning together.

The above image is one of the two key models. They are simple and conceptualize what I have been saying and what we were learning and realizing both as a research group and as an organization. Today, for me, they continue to be a lens (or filter or rule of thumb or guideline) through which I can now view my life and situations. I can determine where and how I am in the model.

This helps me to become more aware, conscious and sensitive to life in and around my context. Thus I move from a more isolated, isolationist, even self-centred perception to a more inclusive one, because more people around me are aware as well. In addition, I become more aware of systems in which I am living – systems which may be healthy or dysfunctional.

The next diagram is an adaptation of the basic model, again, explaining the behaviour associated within each paradigm.

We are often so unaware of the paradigms, systems, or structures within which we live. It is often only when "something happens" that we can or are forced to step back and see our lives from a different perspective. These happenings can be events such as an illness, job loss, financial stress, or relationship breakup, out of which we begin to ask questions – basically contemplating, "What is life about anyway? What can I do differ-

1. OLD PARADIGM-OLD WORLD VIEW
- Dualistic
- Hierarchical
- Either/or thinking
- mechanistic view with
- separate parts
- Individualism
- Dysfunctional systems
- Focused on the self
- Narrow view of reality
- rational objective thought is seen as the only valid way

3. SHIFT to a new paradigm
Willingness to give up fear-filled control . Personal transformation and Transformation of the world

2. lives fragmented - disconnected
- Alienated – detached – chronic disease of our time
- Individual is primary
- Intuition, emotional and artistic expression and experience of the Holy devalued as inauthentic
- Nature to be mastered – resources consumed

A NEW PARADIGM and WORLD VIEW

a new way of living

CONNECTED TO A MUCH LARGER FAMILY
- We are all connected
- We are interconnected
- People are mutually dependent
- Includes all CREATION
- We are all one
- Human species is seen as the consciousness of the cosmos
- Human species has the responsibility to care for the Earth and creation
- Embracing the entire universe
- People live in contemplative awareness
- Life-giving for all
- No split between religion and science
- Relationship is fundamental

ently? What do I really believe?"

Considering the description can be helpful in order to externalize our own feelings and to be able to place ourselves within the models, to help bring some measure of objectivity, external clarity and understanding to our current situations at all levels – in relationships, work situations, family, and church situations (and any other groups of which we may be part.)

The models can help us by naming and describing the variances in each of the aspects of the system of which we are part. By placing ourselves within we can then more easily discover how we want to change, what it means to move to a new paradigm on our journey and where we might be unaware or stuck.

The point though, is that there is no quick fix so that we can change quickly. Rather it is a life long journey moving from being oppressors or victims to people who can live an empowering life with others in relational power – not power *over* people or *under* people, but power *with* others.

Think of it another way. How can I change my paradigm in a world that does not change (or even examine) its paradigm? My ethics, values, morals or beliefs may be different from those around me. Therefore I can find myself at odds with the so-called norm. Do I challenge it or remain passive and victimized? How do I respond?

This transformative change ultimately happens at the deepest levels within us. It is not a technique or something we can just make happen overnight. It is a long, painful, costly journey which requires commitment and staying power and the support of others. It is also social.

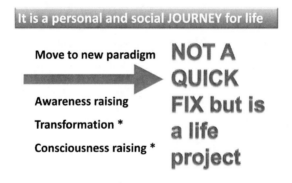

Transformation means alteration, makeover, a complete change, usually into something with an improved appearance or usefulness, according to the Microsoft dictionary.

Consciousness raising (or awareness raising) means having knowledge from having observed something or been told about it, knowing that something exists because you notice it or realize that it is happening. Being well informed about what is going on in the world or about the latest developments in a sphere of activity – this is consciousness raising (according to the Microsoft dictionary).

We also can know by the *fruits* of our lives how we are doing;

that is how we are changing or not, how we are being trans-formed (or not). Again, agape love is measured by the action of good will, kindness, forgiveness and compassion toward others. Love requires constant change and transformation because we never arrive. It is both a feeling and an action.

Our spirituality praxis at personal and social levels results from our practice informing our theory and our theory informing our practice. The result of such an understanding is that it is spirituality in action, grounded and lived out in our daily lives and human actions and in our thoughts, attitudes and beliefs. Again a simple diagram can help us as we place ourselves within it and see what kind of life we are living, noting how we treat others and ourselves. Our spirituality and humanity go together and they cannot be separated – we are who we are; Body, Mind, and Spirit – integrated within ourselves and within the world around us, in our workplace, churches, families, and various groups to which we belong. Our spirituality is not up there or out there, separate from us, simply belonging to and left in church for Sundays or times of personal and private prayer. Rather our spirituality is inside us – is us, our life breath, the animating spirit within, without which we die.

The ways of knowing how we are living and how we can place ourselves on our transformative journeys are by recognizing the signs and fruit of true, authentic spirituality in action.

Being able authentically to live out some or all of the qualities pictured certainly would indicate a measure of spirituality in action. We do not often think of such things in our everyday life. That is, we do not take time to reflect on or slow down long enough to be aware of how we are doing emotionally or spiritually in our relationship with others or ourselves, nor with our own bodies.

As Zohar states, we are spiritually numb or dumb because we have become so desensitized to life, too busy, stressed, under pressure or even confused by so much stimuli and values thrown at us by various media–we just have to switch off. (Zohar 1999))

SIGNS OF SPIRITUALITY IN ACTION

Openness
Respect
Reciprocity
Mutuality
Compassion
Interdependence
Interconnectedness
Interrelationship
Co-operation
A passion for right relationship
Respect for process

If we do take time to stop and think, reflect and meditate however, we realize that most often we have just been triggered by incidents, traumas or difficulties from the past, which we have just come face to face with again. If we know and are aware of the hallmarks or touchstones, then we can evaluate, at least now and again, how far off or how relevant we are living our lives from them. Yet mostly, we are too out of touch, distracted or busy to even notice.

A NON-HIERARCHICAL WEB OF RELATIONSHIPS

Democratic interactive relations
Empowering "with" others
Deep mutual connection
Living with equalness
In solidarity with others especially those who
are oppressed
Recognising "the other"
Democratic interactive relationships
Being able to authentically be able to live
out some or all of the qualities above
certainly would be "spirituality

These ideas have also influenced my own life over the past fourteen years. I particularly find myself using the basic model as a lens to see through, from where I stand, to help me to determine what I am sensing or feeling or to become more consciously aware. Sharing the Models with others then allows us a common visual concept of communication, which helps in our awareness about situations.

I did and still do apply them to my life situations which help me to open my eyes to what is happening and then subsequently make more considered necessary changes.

This living diagrammatic theory is simply a tool which I continue to use in my life; because it includes my spiritual life at a fundamental level, then I live neither as an oppressor or as an oppressed victim.

LIFE IN THE SPIRIT

KNOWING THE SPIRIT WITH:

Head	←→	Heart
Theory	←→	Practice
Both	←→	And

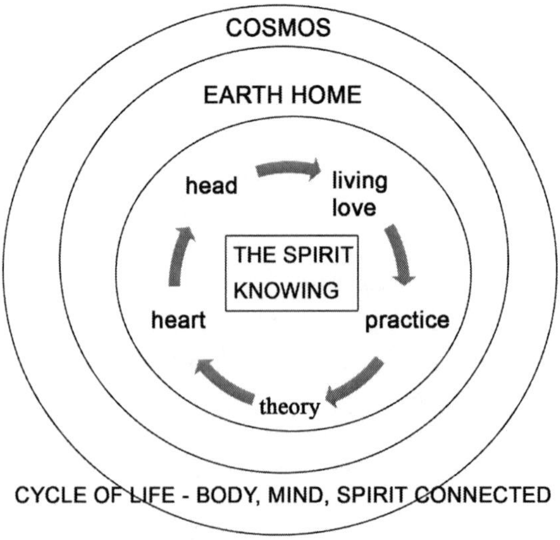

COSMOS

EARTH HOME

head → living love

THE SPIRIT KNOWING

heart practice

theory

CYCLE OF LIFE - BODY, MIND, SPIRIT CONNECTED

Chapter 3

Cycles of Change and Growth

I began this book by asking several people about what they think they have experienced or felt spirituality to be. Some of these people – names anonymous – who are asking the question and searching are religious or churchgoers and some are not. Here are some of the responses:

*   "Spirituality is unique and comes from my spirit and whatever guides me and is more important than religion. It guides my values – values spring from spirituality – what is my spirit is my struggle. I have a 'What do I Believe List.' Spirituality helps me to know who I am versus being a Catholic."
*   "I haven't a clue."
*   "Going deeper into myself in order to be aware of the Divine that is already in me, in order that Divinity might be manifest in the world. I don't connect it with being religious or of Christianity. What pops up is reincarnation; often it leads to a certain view in life as well as how we start and end in life. I think of spirituality as a calling–it is a relaxing word and not a high stress word with open-mindedness to all views of life."
*   "Spirituality means touching base in inner peace, taking moments to connect with your core."
*   "Running through the forest I feel this sense of freedom, accomplishment and power."
*   "Spirituality is my belief system. Religion is '? – based'. I believe Spirituality is knowing everything I need to know. I didn't know why? It's faith in being part of God. I'm as important as God is. If not, then God wouldn't have made

me. And I need to ask for that knowing – that's my prayer. We have to go inside. I know it, I feel it. It's there."

I use the word *praxis* throughout this book. Many people asked me to change the word to *practice* because more persons would find it understandable. Yet, they are not the same thing. The diagram gives further clarification to this concept, which is an on-going process in life. Praxis is practice and theory informing each other mutually.

The Cycle of Growth

The spiritual journey does not take place as quickly as the flight of an arrow. Life isn't like that; rather we find ourselves living through cycles of change and growth – needing to complete all the aspects or stages of each of the cycles in turn. Life is a process, from beginning to end and it is up to us personally to choose how we will live it out in action, giving expression in those relationships in our lives, both personal and social.

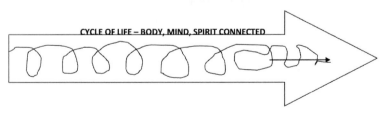

CYCLE OF LIFE – BODY, MIND, SPIRIT CONNECTED

The journey of transformation is necessary and difficult for all individuals, organizations, at personal and social levels. It requires conscious discernment and awareness at every level and point and doesn't just happen. We connect our inner and outer realities and concerns.

Many others in the field of spirituality have researched and written now since the awareness of spirituality has increased in the academy in the late 1990's. It is important to be cognizant of some of their voices, concerns and findings. Further research is needed in order to have an authentic and inclusive under-standing of spirituality. If we make the journey, there are resultant attributes which can be recognised within the authentic spirituality worldview.

At its simplest, the cycle of growth can be reduced to five stages:

* I have an *experience.*
* I *reflect* on that experience.
* I *express* my experience in words.
* I make *sense* of my experience.
* I decide what *action* will come out of this process.
* (And then I begin another cycle...)

For example, I need or want to make a decision about what response I could have after seeing the on-going scenes on television about the devastating drought in Somalia. My heart and feelings have been touched and continue to be each time I see more news or talk about it with others. I begin to reflect on my deep and impacting experience and try to make sense of them in relationship to my own life here and now today. What can I do? Is there any helpful response I can make? Once I make a decision about what I can do, I take action: make a donation, pray for the situation and people, or invite others to join me in prayer or in gathering some funds or clothing.

Spirituality is not just about me but is about others/us, where and how we live as one.

The Dynamic of Discernment

The Dynamic of Discernment outlines this life cycle or process.

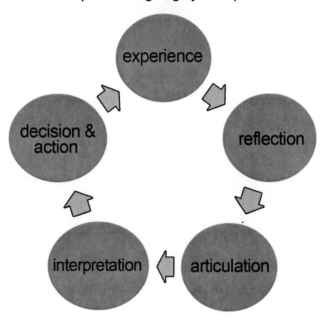

DYNAMIC OF DISCERNMENT
A five-phase on-going cyclical process

According to Coghlan, discernment is both individual and communal.

* *Experience* – Personal experience is the starting point of spiritual discernment because that is where our Higher Power is recognised.
* *Reflection* – we reflect on what has taken place throughout the period being examined. We examine how we are being moved in relation to other persons.
* *Articulation* – is significant since people attempt to express

what happened to them. Others can interact and thus help to draw out the deeper significance of what is being shared. Language is important and such interchange can help interpret the experience and implications for the future. Disclosure actually helps to bring about community and helps it also to develop and grow.

* *Interpretation* – the formal moment of discernment, the activity by which we recognise the significance of our inner experience. This includes further understanding in relation to the present or future decision and action.

* *Decision-and-action* – necessarily follow the interpretation and if they do not then the previous phases are a sham. Reflection thus moves to action. (Coghlan and Brannick 2001)

The whole of the process has to be kept in mind since each phase interacts with the others. The process is cyclical and the cycles can happen very quickly so it is difficult to recognise when one begins and another lets off. The cycle is a way of life.

The experience of action introduces a new cycle of the five phases and continual use of this five-phase cycle develops the spirituality of discernment as a way of life. The purposes of discernment are: communal well-being and self-knowledge, awareness of the felt presence of the Divine and the response to the Spirit of the Divine/Unnameable moving the person or group forward.

Time is needed for private meditation, prayer, reflection and perhaps followed by discussion and sharing. Time is also necessary for understanding the significance of the experiences for subsequent decision-making. A spiritual guide is helpful in this process to assist discernment. (English 1992: 29-41)

The cycle outlined is important and similar to the learning cycle. It is also used extensively in theories of change. Often many people want to get on with the task and action and so miss out the middle three aspects of the cycle of: *reflection, articulation, and interpretation* and instead, they end up going round and round in the same place in a vicious circle rather than in a progressive change cycle. They don't want to take time for reflection or discernment, perhaps not even knowing how to live through those stages.

In this busy twenty-first century most of us want to rush on. We think we already have too much "to do" without "wasting" time, in taking even more time in reflecting and conceptualizing – that is picturing, imagining or perceiving something. Although the process of growth and change is the same, we call it discernment in the area of spirituality.

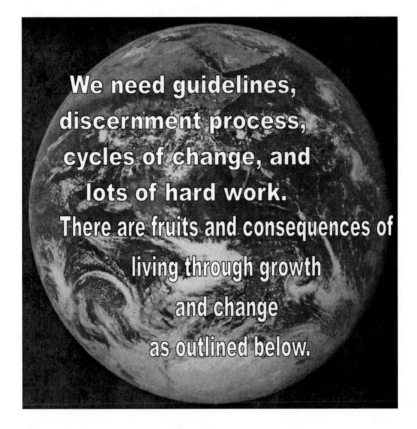

We need guidelines,
discernment process,
cycles of change, and
lots of hard work.
There are fruits and consequences of
living through growth
and change
as outlined below.

The Social Aspects of Discernment

Discernment is making a judgement or discrimination; it is demonstrating shrewdness. We have already talked about Spirituality being personal and social since we are all part of one whole. Here I want to focus on the social aspects of discernment.

A major shift or change in our personal and social lives is required so we can embrace a wider reality which is fundamental to authentic spirituality. I have previously referred to the inner and outer aspects of living our spirituality, realizing that they are connected and *not* separate. We probably know this at some level, but sometimes putting this concept or understanding into diagrammatic form helps us to connect with what is being felt, experienced and so being able to name and own how we live with more understanding and choice.

SOCIAL ASPECT OF THE MODEL

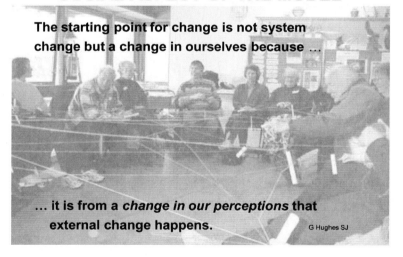

The starting point for change is not system
change but a change in ourselves because ...

... it is from a *change in our perceptions* that
external change happens.   G Hughes SJ

CONNECTING INNER AND OUTER SPIRITUALITY

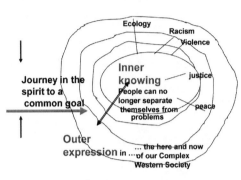

- integrate inner knowing and outer expression

- find ways to live spiritual journey

- authentic spiritual life must be fulfilled here and now in place we live

- not enough to recognize spiritual longing our hearts need to be renewed

These problems can only be solved at the level of Spirit **not of the mind**. The goal of each religion is the same so we can join hands in this journey toward a common goal and so experience unity in diversity. A challenge to the institutional religions. (Johnson 2000:84)

The diagram above names a few of our common human problems, which surround us in our wider context, and affects our personal lives too. We have inner knowing and as that awareness grows, we begin to realise that our spiritual journey which includes the whole of our life, requires us to be responsible and authentic in the context in which we live.

That context is immediate and local but also global and everything in between. We see and hear about our world every day on the radio and television, in newspapers and magazines. Many now make the statement that our world is getting smaller and smaller. We can feel and experience what others are going through across the world through the ever-increasing expertise of media communication. For instance, many of us around the world have been seeing on television in our global home, the terrible scenes of starvation and death played out in our own living rooms. It continues to be a global event that we share just as it is happening in front of our very eyes and hearts.

The discernment model helps us in our personal lives to understand and develop spirituality praxis. It also helps in our social ethics and life in part because our inner and outer lives are connected. In fact, inner- and outer-knowing as well as change can't be separated and requires a journey at both individual and social levels. (Lorimer, 1998)

As we take time for our spiritual work using self-reflective consciousness and discernment, with awareness of what is going on both within and outside of ourselves, our understanding evolves into a greater awareness of the world. (O'Murchu, 2002)

Action orientated spirituality incorporates:

* action *and* contemplation
* social *and* personal worlds
* outward *and* inward
* personal *and* political permeation where discrimination, disadvantage, domination, and oppression in society are *replaced* by empowerment and enabling.

Global concerns and issues today have escalated. People have become more fearful and worried for themselves, their families, and the whole of our world. The old dominant systems have led our world to its present state. Transformation is needed at all levels.

Dynamic of discernment
A five phase on-going cyclical process

Old paradigm
Oppressive systems
Out dated God images

... At personal, social, global levels so that we can live out a NEW PARADIGM as changed people in our Earth Home

- Environment
- Global warming
- Terrorism
- Health Fears
- Health issues
- Stress
- Earthquakes
- Financial
- Political

We can continue to add many other current concerns as they develop each day it seems; for instance, there are now so many more floods, fires, earthquakes, toxic spills of various sorts, new viruses and pests and very unpredictable weather, accompanied by increased and unprecedented acts of social violence in so many countries.

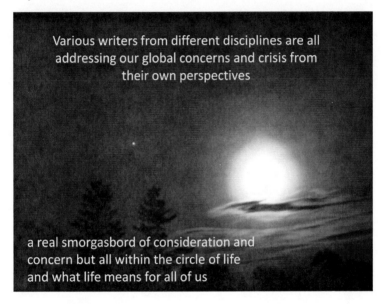

Various writers from different disciplines are all addressing our global concerns and crisis from their own perspectives

a real smorgasbord of consideration and concern but all within the circle of life and what life means for all of us

Now, in some ways, people – that is, activists, academics, scientists, theologians, economists, business people, cosmologists, environmentalists, educators, health providers and so many others – are saying the same thing in seemingly small and yet significant ways. That is, "things" need to change because we are on a pathway to destruction at so many levels within our earth home.

There are so many opinions, suggestions, books, articles, television programmes and research findings emerging, mostly saying the same thing from within their own disciplines and observations. They are all concerned with spirituality and are teaching about it, writing about it, and theorising about how spirituality relates to and is significant to their own disciplines and how it can be integrated and incorporated and added onto what they already know. Often their deliberations happen without previous experience or informed study in the field of spirituality.

The concern is that an adequate spirituality theory is missing especially because spirituality is still a varied and misunderstood word with many definitions, meanings, and beliefs. Without some comprehensive academic study accompanied by some practice or experience, they would be unable to join their various disciplines together.That presents problems. Within

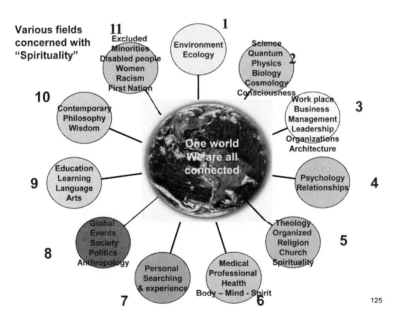

academia spirituality is still considered a subsection of the theology department. It does not have its own department much in the same way that the discipline of psychology was tucked into other departments in the 1950s. There remains, therefore, a lack of consistency, oversight, research or shared understanding within both the field or discipline of spirituality and with its own internal and varying differences, which are many.

An added problem is that various disciplines can develop their own perspectives and methods for incorporating spirituality into their discipline. Each definition is presented as valid, authentic and relevant to people who wouldn't perceive inconsistency and can then be misled or confused.

For example, check out recent books on the market on spirituality and

* Psychology
* Business
* the Workplace
* Organisations
* Environment
* Health
* Science
* Chicken soup

This would not occur in the field of, say psychology today, because the discipline would have challenged the development and integration of psychology by all those other disciplines.

Spirituality is a minefield, or perhaps better, a smorgasbord with an ever-changing understanding. The Spirit does not want to be put in a box. No one religion or discipline has an exclusive theory or ownership of spirituality. It is still an elusive, growing, expanding and mysterious field. The Divine, Other, Higher Power is not a discipline or theory but an experience of a living Reality. It is not yet another dogma or theory or fad or quick fix to feeling better.

Definitions, Concerns, and Cautions

The comments below outline the thinking, perspective and concerns of people involved in the field of spirituality:

It is extremely important to hear and consider what they are saying with their very strong voices, so that we can ensure that an understanding of "spirituality" doesn't become inauthentic because of the lack of research and by "not" listening to the voices of those who have been engaged in it for decades. Hence, I have included their comments in this book, for all to consider and learn from.

It seemed that the more I studied and learned within the field, which also "requires" appropriation (application), the more I became concerned and could see more and more discrepancies, in more and more places and levels. And so it goes on. People get caught in that web of confusion. We are all one, and we do have different experiences, perspectives and belief systems. I did do "Doctoral" level research, over a period of four years, within the specific research context explained above; never-the-less, I became increasingly aware that we were not isolated as a research team, in the social sense and that that was not possible in such a field of research as "spirituality praxis". There are other academics considering the same subject both academically and experientially and so it seems utterly important and essential to include in our "research" what others were also "researching", considering and finding elsewhere.

I have included a very brief summary of some of those findings below, so that the reader can also have a broader consideration and view.

Others offer cautions to seekers and consumers:

"The word 'spirituality' is in vogue and keeps appearing in novels, plays and films, political manifestos, government and education papers, in business and industry boardrooms. Bookshops have larger sections dealing with spirituality than with religion, often with a popular section labelled, 'the Occult.' Besides the occult, there are a bewildering variety of spiritualities on offer. How are we to find our way among competing and conflicting spiritualities?" Gerard Huges is a Jesuit in the UK (2002)

Higgins and Letson write that: "We are in a transition from a former world which bores us, to a coming one which numbs us with uncertainty". They say that one clear sign of this uncertainty and its attendant anxiety can be found in the significant rise of interest in spirituality. People are drawn in increasing numbers to explore the many complex and exciting areas of interconnection between spirituality and other areas of human endeavour and meaning. The new frontiers of knowledge so boldly pioneered by scientists and the new technology elites have opened up grand vistas of challenge and concern for the devout, the questing and the curious.

They caution that we need guides, a discourse and a map that will allow them entrée into a world more foreign than that of the microbe, the megabyte and the mutual fund. The thirst for a meaningful or living spirituality is unquenchable and there are not a few purveyors of the "spiritual arts" willing to peddle their dubious wares at a speedy rate and at cut-rate costs. Need is occasionally known to generate desperation and the snake oil person is quick to rise to the entrepreneurial challenge. Higgins and Letson point out that some who have lived out a spirituality journey believe that a genuine spirituality of resistance grounded in a love both for justice and for the contemplative dimension, will have little time for the easy spiritualities that are so effort-lessly marketed in Western culture as the next phases in self-fulfilment. "The Chicken Soup for the Soul" school of spirituality espouses a strategy of self-enhancement techniques, a feel-good process of self-affirmation that appeals to the contemporary readers, hungry for spiritual fulfilment but disinclined to struggle for spiritual enlightenment. They add that an alternative knowing that spirituality which is communal, historical, and theological, with justice as part of its very definition is a spirituality best poised to thrive in the new century, which is not self-occupied and insular. (Higgins and Letson 2002)

There are more than fifty-seven spiritualities and a widespread interest in spirituality along with misunderstandings, distortions, and grandiose claims. Cashmore and Puls (2000) suggest that we search for a healthy and a more deeply integrated practice rather than one that is too individualistic and focussed on individual inwardness. It is important to know therefore who it is who is actually defining spirituality.

Abram believes that a contemporary spirituality challenges us to reclaim connections to recover, resume, redeem, heal and repair rents in the fabric of our world, so that we can all live together as one family in a reconciled new creation. (Abram 1996.)

Cavanaugh gives an overview of current thought about understanding new spirituality in business pointing out that it means different things to different people. He points out that sixty percent of people are positive towards spirituality and negative towards organized religion which has had an impact on how spirituality has developed with no one dominant religion, hence neither in spirituality in the workplace. (Cavanaugh, 2000)

Schneiders states that people often have a vague, uninformed, shallow and shapeless generalized ethos or instead of that of the extremism and instability of cults. "The term spirituality is used so indiscriminately today, that it risks losing all specific meaning." (Schneiders, 1999)

Downey states that we are spiritually ill as a result of our fragmented post-modern thinking and being. The soul sickness that people experience as they yearn and search for "something more" is not only on at a personal level but also at corporate levels with an accompanying spiritual and social crisis. The subsequent tidal wave of interest has now afforded us a smorgasbord of various styles of spirituality, which can be very confusing. However, because there is still a lack of precision about what people mean when they speak about spirituality, he thinks we need a definition that allows "enough room" for all that is authentic in the quest for the sacred. (Downey, 1997)

Clouser recognises people think that they have no religious belief when they actually do, that they have unconscious assumptions or that many actually call it by another name, thereby disguising its religious character. He emphasizes that religious belief cannot be walled off from the rest of knowledge since it is actually one of the most influential beliefs we hold, affecting our conceptions of human nature and destiny and ideas of society, justice, ethics and science. (Clouser, 1999)

Lorimer writes that the consciousness of the experimenter affects the experiment – hence the importance of scientists and the mystics coming together to discuss similarities in their twin approaches to truth and knowledge. He believes that it is even more important to transform that knowledge into experience. Today, scientists with only a modicum of self-knowledge are working with vast creative as well as potentially destructive powers in many fields. Mystics can help them gain the wisdom that is so necessary. (Lorimer, 2000)

Zohar, a physicist, states that the radically new science of the twentieth century is more compatible with our spiritual intuitions... taking its insights on board may actually help us to articulate a more modern spiritual and moral vision. (Zohar, 1994) She also points out that we are spiritually dumb, alienated, fragmented, disconnected and often narcissistic, ego-centred and individualistic in our search for meaning and purpose. (Zohar, 2000)

Ken Wilber and Fr Thomas Keating dialogue on -You-Tube: http://thesethingsinside.wordpress.com/2011/05/11/ken-wilber-and-thomas-keating-discuss-integral-spirituality

Douglas Burton Christie believes that spirituality has a wide berth since it refers to "the experience of consciously striving to integrate one's life in terms, not of isolation and self-absorption but of self-transcendence toward the ultimate value one perceives...it is understood to be inclusive of the widest possible range of human experience ...is more inclusive and elastic...it is the whole of one's emotions and behaviour in respect to what is ultimate...is holistic, encompassing all one's relationships to all of creation – to the self, and to others, to society and nature, to work and leisure – in a fundamentally spiritual or religious orientation." (Burton-Christie, 1994)

Smith wrote that the mechanical worldview is no longer adequate for our times and we recognise that we are all caught up in the pursuit of a more united world, a more harmonious way of life; a movement towards wholeness, non-dualism and inclusiveness. (Smith, 2000)

We all have our own problems and concerns for our earth home. We are all part of its life. Teilhard de Chardin wrote about such awareness as well. Therefore, although we consider spiritual awareness and are learning about current concerns we can learn from his writings from many years ago; they are still very relevant.

THE PLANET

- Since we live in an evolving universe the PROBLEM is not to protect the possessions of the individual

- So much as to guide the person to wholeness in order that the spiritual energies of the planet may reach their highest development

Teilhard de Chardin

I offer the tree image again because it depicts various aspects involved in our growth and change. It requires deep learning, is a mystery, theory and practice which when combined can change us. Awareness at various levels is important; we also need guidelines and way-markers for our journey so we do not get lost or too confused.

There is a significant amount of fruit that emerges as we do our hard work of hanging in with our consciousness and transformative process and don't stop along our path or journey and give up. We can live with more love and freedom, and with justice and inclusion. It is important to walk our own talk, in being and embodied in our way of life. It is not through living out theory or techniques, but who we are being.

Living together in our cosmos and interconnected universe, we are now beginning to realize that we are all deeply interconnected. We also are becoming more aware of how we are experiencing power, dualism, greed and attachment. Our past conditioning with its own individual histories and roots, has left us with various prejudices about which we now need to become

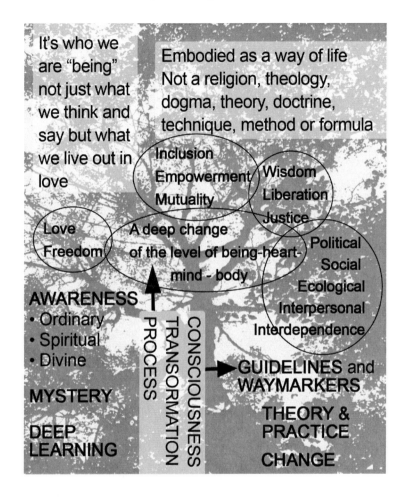

It's who we are "being" not just what we think and say but what we live out in love

Embodied as a way of life Not a religion, theology, dogma, theory, doctrine, technique, method or formula

Inclusion
Empowerment
Mutuality

Wisdom
Liberation
Justice

Love
Freedom

A deep change of the level of being-heart-mind - body

Political
Social
Ecological
Interpersonal
Interdependence

AWARENESS
• Ordinary
• Spiritual
• Divine

MYSTERY

DEEP LEARNING

PROCESS
TRANSFORMATION
CONSCIOUSNESS

GUIDELINES and WAYMARKERS

THEORY & PRACTICE

CHANGE

aware and then to own as we journey on our life-long path of transformation. We have also inherited and learned many healthy caring attributes which we still live out.

Some of those attributes, we can marshal to make changes, in order to be able to live in the circle of mutuality. The cost for each journey is immense of course and varies according to our individual pasts. We need to become aware and conscious, so we can unlearn before we can re-learn and choose to change. It takes commitment, determination and hard work.

ATTRIBUTES OF THE JOURNEY

MOVE FROM DOMINATION

↓

Own the pain and actively appropriate the experience of love during the transformation

Both categories perish and are

➤

demolished into the new order of participation

↑

MOVE FROM SUBMISSION

• oppression,
• exploitation
• Experiences of pain, domination,
• Recognizing a dissonance between what is and what ought to be

Understanding "Personal is political" challenges us to transform human relationships and institutions and to restructure in accordance to equal humanity and the integrity of all people.

Recover and release repressed energies which have been violated by the surrounding culture and therefore split off from consciousness and submerged in the psyche.

Belief systems and day to day practices have imprisoned us all in roles which deny humanity.

Those who then make this journey are participants of the most universal social change. In fact the survival of the world order is at stake as we struggle to rescue ourselves.

The fruit is that the goal of replacing individualism with love will have been achieved.

Our idea of God needs to undergo transformation with a radical redefinition of God. just changing the language is confusing and unsatisfactory... The incomprehensible God transcends and transforms present images and symbols so we can internalize and relocate and reinterpret this God of love,

In this contemplative love, not given on demand, and experienced beyond conscious control we are purified from projections. Then we can give theology the insights it needs to search out new doctrines of God.

We realize that we can live out this change when we are able to love others more deeply as more integrated, whole and complete persons.

God is a mystery, Presence, Power, Love . God and love are inseparable – it is not possible to tear them apart. God is our capacity to love and is the power and spark that animates our love.

The new paradigm is one of participation where the whole pattern of domination is demolished – The new paradigm of sharing one body, one life, mutual selfhood as friends.

The new paradigm is one of participation where the whole pattern of domination is demolished The new paradigm is sharing one body, one life, mutual selfhood as friends

Spirituality Is about Others as Well as You

My own learning came from some of the research and development I did, learning with others, not top-down, which used to be the preferred way, but instead using the tree-metaphor within the group. We were all learning, contributing, and researching together. The process also required me, as ethnographer-researcher living in the midst of and being part of the research, to stay objective, to take my hands off and not impose my ideas or direction on the group. It truly was a process in which we were not aiming for a particular outcome, but were willing to stay within the cycles and let the outcome emerge as a result of the process.

A SUMMARY IMAGE

Who you are

You are not just your "self".
You are joined and bound
together with many other
"selves" – all linked into
one – into Love. Nothing
and no one is separate
But all are part of the vast
canvas called life on Earth

All on the same page, all
on the same planet/Globe,
all living on the same Earth
Home Community
All breathing the same air,
sharing the same stars,
sun, moon, water and food
and all resources in our
shared home.
The same energy, light,
love and Spirit, Creator –
all living in a vast web of
relationships.

You are who you are
And you live in a local and
global context and milieu,
family, society, nation,
environment, government,
church, shaped and
influenced by them.
BODY, MIND AND SPIRIT

**You can "choose"
always**

With growing openness,
consciousness, change,
transformation and
awareness which is either
ordinary, spiritual or
divine, we perceive light
or dark, love or hate, life
or death, positive or
negative.

Life is non-linear, evolving
in a process and journeys

Part Two

Science Supports Spirituality

Chapter 4

Dipping into Quantum Mechanics

In the previous chapter, I argued that spirituality is its own intellectual and research subject, not a component of the philosophy, psychology or theology departments. In this chapter, I want to underscore my assertion by showing, as simply as I can, how Quantum Science (which is what I am terming quantum mechanics and quantum physics) supports spirituality as a discipline.

I began this work in 1998 and found it so exciting and relevant to spirituality that I could not understand what kept everyone from jumping up and down. My academic mentor said that it takes time for people to catch on. Mind, Body, and Spirit (MBS) folks picked up its implications soon afterward, and this may have prevented the spirituality academics from moving quickly.

Scientific Starts

In the 1600s, physicist Isaac Newton invented the clock and along with it, his mechanistic understanding of science. The main features of this science are cause and effect, predictability, rules, laws and order, certainty. All aspects of life were influenced by and caught up in this new science and worldview: church institutions, education, medicine, nature, art, politics, business, and relationships – like cogs in a wheel. The industrialized age also came into being, which seemed a great advantage to bring order – a clockwork life in which people knew where they were and what to expect.

About 100 years ago, several scientists and physicists began to discover that those previous findings of Newton's were not complete. There are other realities in quantum science –almost the reverse understanding and findings. In quantum science there is chaos, no order or predictability; we all have choices, belong together in a web of relationships; power is seen as power *with* others, not over or under others, including ourselves. Our earth home by now has suffered great damage and abuse at the hands of the clock-maker model. Land is now desecrated, rivers and lakes polluted, the greenhouse effect growing, polluted air worldwide, even the educational, medical, and religious institutions have been converted to clockwork ideals.

Most physicists do not totally agree with one another or use different terms for the same thing, so this makes explaining physics quickly even more difficult. I chose physicist Danah Zohar's writing after having read her work as I began my research into spirituality. Her work links our lives and makes the relationship between them relevant to everyday life. She also explores ensuing implications in a way that helps strengthen the connection between science and spirituality. Rather than trying to explain more on quantum science here, I have summarized some of her work because of its great clarity and inclusiveness. Readers still may need to make more than one reading to be able to see all the connections, but certainly it is worth the effort. In fact, deeper reflection on this understanding will result in deeper learning and help us in our much needed "radical turn around" and paradigm change.

Zohar, *The Quantum Self*, on Quantum Science

She asks questions at the outset, such as:

* Who am I?
* Why am I here?
* What is my place in the scheme of things?
* Why is the world like it is?
* What does it mean that one day I must die?

These are some of the key questions of urgency that many of us have, often with no real answers.

Quantum science shows us that we cannot separate ourselves from our environment. More importantly, she claims, the insights of physics can illuminate our understanding of everyday life and help us to better understand our relationship to ourselves, others, and the world at large.

The book's central theme is about how to get beyond a particular form of alienation that has plagued life in this century, to such an extent that we have become strangers in this universe. To do this she looks at the relationship between matter and consciousness in quantum theory, and proposes a new quantum mechanical theory of consciousness that promises to bring us back into partnership with the universe.

Zohar states that the roots of our alienation run deep in our culture going back as far as Plato's philosophy, in which distinctions were made between the world of ideas and experience. However, the strongest influences were from the seventeenth century with the cultivation of René Descartes' philosophy of doubt – "How do I know that I exist? I think, therefore, I am" – and the birth of Newtonian or classical physics. Both of them radically changed the way we look at ourselves and our relationship to our world. That is Cartesian philosophy wrenched us from familiar social and religious context and thrust us into "I-centred culture", which is dominated by egocentricity and overemphasis on 'I' and 'mine'. Conversely, the living cosmos during Greek and Medieval times was filled with purpose and intelligence driven by the love of God for the benefit of humanity. Again Newton's thinking tore us out from the fabric of the universe itself with an entirely lifeless design – a dead clockwork machine. Rules in this world were fixed and determined; human beings and the whole of consciousness and life itself were irrelevant to the working of his vast universal machine.

Then for 300 or so years, our lives have been coloured by this bleak Newtonian vision. This has given rise to unyielding despair in our alien and inhuman world. Therefore, to a large extent we have not been able to preserve our aspirations because morally, spiritually and aesthetically our culture seems to be under stress. We often find ourselves grounded in nothing larger than ourselves, becoming makers of our own values, guardians of our own conscience, and indifferent to what seems like "the dead God". (Nietzsche)

So much of modern sociology, educational theory and psychology of the persona follows from such thinking – as does our current violence, a natural reaction to so much impotence. Our attitude to nature is equally affected; we are set apart from and in opposition to our material environment. We have set out to conquer nature, to overwhelm her and use her for our own needs which end up with the desecration of the environment.

A mindless proliferation of ugly, manufactured, material structures easily follows on then from this sense of alienation from Nature. Although the old Newtonian worldview often and unknowingly still dominates our lives, we now have the new physics which is Einstein's relativity theory and quantum mechanics.

Quantum physics is about that tiny micro-world within the atom, describing the inner workings of everything we see and at least physically are. It states that nothing in particular can be said to exist in any fixed place and everything is awash in a sea of possibilities. Some scientists deny that there is any reality at all. Zohar believes that we human beings are the natural bridge between the everyday world and the world of Quantum physics. She also believes that a closer look at the nature and role of consciousness will lead both to a deeper philosophical under-standing of the everyday and to a more complete picture of quantum theory.

She believes that consciousness, like matter, emerges from the world of quantum events, that the two, though wholly different from each other, have a common mother in quantum reality. Our thought patterns and our relationships – to ourselves, to others, and to the world at large – might in some ways be explained by and in other ways mirror the same laws and behaviour patterns that govern the world of electrons and protons.

What is at stake here? If our intellect does draw its laws from nature, then our perception of these laws must to some degree mirror the reality of nature herself. In knowing ourselves, we can come to know nature. She believes that through wedding physics, science, quantum physics and our psychology, we can live in a reconciled universe in which our culture and we are fully and meaningfully part of the scheme of things.

Now let me summarize Zohar's writing as she explains the basic notions of being, movement and relationship in quantum physics.

Being: The most revolutionary concept is the wave-particle duality, because it asserts that all being at the subatomic level can be described equally well either as *solid particles*, like minute billiard balls, or as *waves*, like undulations on the surface of the sea. However neither description is accurate on its own, since *both* the wave-like and the particle-like aspects of being must be considered together when trying to understand the nature of things; quantum 'stuff' is essentially *both* wave-like *and* particle-like simultaneously. Each is a way that matter can manifest itself and both together are what matter *is*. While neither state is complete in itself, both are necessary to give us a complete picture of reality.

Movement: At a quantum level, the whole picture of continuous movement through space and time breaks down. All energy is radiated in individual packets called 'quanta' rather than in flowing streams over a continuous spectrum. Electrons jump from one energy state to another in discontinuous 'quantum leaps' – the size of the leap depending on how many quanta of energy they have absorbed or given off. Things can happen in any direction since a transition is largely a matter of chance – time reversibility at quantum level – there is no familiar succession of events within the disturbed atom, with one thing causing another; things just happen as they happen. It tries out, all at once, all the possible new orbits into which it might eventually settle, in much the same way that we might try out a new idea by throwing out imaginary scenarios, depicting as many possible consequences.

Relationship: Perhaps more than anything else quantum physics promises to transform our notions of relationship. Both the concept of *"being"* as an indeterminate wave/particle dualism and a concept of *"movement"* which rests on virtual transitions leads to a revolution in our perception of how things relate. Things and events once conceived of as separate, parted in both space and time, are seen by quantum theorists as so integrally linked that their bond mocks the reality of both space and time. They behave instead as multiple aspects of some larger whole, their individual existences deriving both their definition and their meaning from that whole; it follows as a direct consequence of the wave/particle dualism. If all potential things stretch out infinitely in all directions, how does one speak of any distance between them, or conceive of any separateness? All things and all moments touch each other at every point; the oneness of the overall system is paramount. One body can influence another instantaneously, despite there being no apparent exchange of force or energy. It is a fact so alien to space and the time framework of our everyday reality that it remains one of the greatest conceptual challenges raised by quantum theory. Instantaneous action at a distance or "non-locality" – has obvious mystical overtones. It flies in the face of common sense just as does the example of a butterfly's wings influencing the weather in South Africa.

Physically Interwoven: Zohar suggests that there is an underlying *physical* basis for the moral imperative of the Golden Rule: "to do unto others as I would have them do unto me". "Understanding the extent to which we are physically interwoven requires a revolution in our whole way of perceiving ourselves and our relation to others," interwoven into a tapestry of interwoven partnership.

When I first read Zohar's book, *The Quantum Self*, in 1998 I found it extremely and overwhelmingly exciting and still do since she appears to open up completely new ways of perceiving the physical basis for understanding self, relationships and immortality. In particular she believes that an understanding of the quantum nature of person can give us a new paradigm for how human beings function. It all depends on our own personal deepening relationship, commitment and responsibility to others. However all of this requires a radical turnaround from our present *egocentric* alienated way of looking at things.

Implications of Quantum Physics in Our Lives Today

The physics of human consciousness emerges from the quantum process within the brain. Consequently human consciousness shares physics with everything else in this universe. It becomes impossible to imagine a single aspect of our lives that is not drawn into one coherent whole. This physics is the basis for understanding relationship with ourselves, with others and with God/Divine or Other. This understanding allows us to see ourselves and our souls as full partners in the process of nature, helping us to see how we relate to everything else in the universe.

Often the lives of many people are a picture of dissolution; morally, spiritually and aesthetically – where we ourselves are grounded in nothing larger than ourselves. With a spiritually barren life, the souls of modern people cry out for something beyond selves.

So, how can quantum physics help in this desperate situation in which we find ourselves? What is the relevance with the tiny micro-world within the atom, which describes the inner workings of everything we see and physically are? This relevance provides us with a radically new understanding of our physical and human world, particularly through a new physics of consciousness.

Everything and everyone is so integrally linked that all talk of individuals or separation is a distortion of the truth or an illusion. The unity of consciousness with the undivided wholeness of all things, transcends our separation from each other and the world at large. The human being is a tiny microcosm of cosmic being. We are made of the same stuff and held together by the same dynamics as everything else in the universe and vice versa.

Quantum Memory

With this 'insight' the past is 'now' and the past and present are transformed and form a new way forward. The quantum self is a more fluid self, changing and evolving at every moment. To know fully the person I am, I must understand the relationships that I am, the wave aspect of my being. Zohar believes that the self and relationships, the "I" and "we", is not *either/or* but *both/and*. We can now ground this reality in the new physical conceptual structure for interpersonal relationships, which is as we have seen, now understood to be based on the physics of consciousness.

The *"particle" aspect* as we have seen gives rise to individuals and can assign identity. The *"wave" aspect* gives rise to relationships between individuals.

The relationships between you and me then become "we," presenting the same for interpersonal relationships. It is non-local overlap across time. Zohar believes there is definitely a physical basis for interpersonal relationship which is demonstrated in the uncanny way in which quantum mechanics fits what we already know, saying if I can be a self in the first place, a self-for-myself, I can then be a self with and for others and it is impossible otherwise in the quantum model.

Quantum Immortality and Relationship

The quantum vacuum exists eternally, underlying all. That is where all basic properties are conserved so each quantum event leaves its footprints in the sands of time. Our past is alive and is always a living presence woven into now, relived afresh at each moment. The past influences the present and the present impinges on the past. Through intimacy, we are intertwined.

Zohar calls this ground state the coherent quantum vacuum, which contains within itself all potentiality, and which we can conceive of as God/The Other/Mystery/the Unnameable/Divine or whatever we call that which is other than us, not in the empirical world around us.

We truly understand our place in the evolving universe as we see ourselves as thoughts in the mind of God, with each of us living our lives therefore within a cosmic context. Everything each of us does affects all of the rest of us directly. No choice is without significance for the rest of life. Each choice also has an influence on the next one, because it either increases or decreases the probability flow. People, for instance, who act against all odds, are heroes who made hard choices that make it easier for others then because of the physics of the quantum interconnectedness of our consciousness.

We also need to be aware that habit is a free ride because it requires little mental work and is an escape clause for the lazy, because it saves the energy. It is a time when we don't act therefore out of freedom nor do we experience our creativity and we have little psychic growth. The point is that we are tempted to conform to accepted codes of behaviour or adhere to strictly defined codes of duty, thereby avoiding spending our energy or taking time for reflection and discernment so that we can make our own relevant and appropriate choices and decisions.

Chapter 5

Seeking an Authentic Spirituality

Quantum reality and vision depends on our deepening relationship to others, because we believe that "I am my relationships." This requires a radical turnaround from the usual egocentric self-centred way of looking at life. Commitment is a driving force binding us to any relationship. We are entangled, correlated, interwoven, and have potential for more entanglement and deeper relationships. I am my brother's/sister's keeper because my brother or sister is part of me."Human beings create, think and become individuated, independent creatures only within and through a context of meaningful relations to other human beings and to non-human beings." We are all stitches in the same fabric and in hurting others, I hurt myself.

Key Similarities and Overlaps between Spirituality and Quantum Science

With the quantum view, we understand the extent to which we are all physically interwoven and this requires a revolution in our whole way of perceiving ourselves and our relations to others, which happens firstly with our understanding and then letting it resonate with what we already know and live. We can then decide how to be responsible and to be able to have a generative influence on spirituality today as we seek to live out the "revolution"in our whole way of perceiving ourselves with our relationships to others in the past, present and future. All of this can happen only, of course, if we practice what is suggested, allowing it to impact and transform our lives.

Much hard work is required to keep relationships working yet Zohar believes that we will be able to live as one with the universe, living in a reconciled and integrated way within our selves, others and the universe. As she has stated commitment is important and it takes energy to keep making decisions to keep in relationship with another, and the longer we are involved in any sort of intimacy the more we are changed as is the other.

Zohar writes as a physicist, and as with any new science or framework presented, it takes a period of time for people to embrace and accept the implications in order to actualise its meaning. We need to unlearn and relearn a new way of being and knowing.

I believe that when trying to learn or embrace new concepts or information it is sometimes useful to have it written out in succinct point form, by way of a summary of all that has been written and read. I have done just that below, pointing out and highlighting the fundamental understanding, which has been written above.

1. In the quantum model everything is connected.
2. Relationships are important and they are not seen as separate things and events, parted in time and space but instead are integrally linked.
3. We see ourselves and our purposes as part of the universe. Thus we come to understand the meaning of

human existence, where we are here in this material universe.

4. We human beings share some of our nature with all other creatures.

5. The quantum vacuum contains within itself all potentiality. The evolutionary process is a quantum process – if it leads to a greater ordered coherence we will succeed as a species, if not we will fail.

6. Through the decisions or actions we take, a thread draws seemingly disparate pieces together into a coherent whole.

7. We must therefore be in touch with our own experiences and deepest intuitions to have knowledge of the world and ourselves.

8. Quantum physics gives a physical basis to a more holistic, less fragmented way of looking at ourselves; the whole world of creation shares physics with everything else in the universe.

9. The human being is a tiny microcosm of a cosmic being – we are made of the same stuff and held together by the same dynamics as everything else in the universe.

10. The "I" and the "we" is "both/and" in the new physics of consciousness. "I" and "you" become "we".

11. The quantum vacuum exists eternally, underlying all. Our past is alive and always a living presence woven into the now, relived afresh at every moment.

12. Who I am now arises from a tapestry of interwoven patterns in the quantum system of my brain and I am also I-and-you, within time and beyond.

13. We are only in an intimate relationship to the extent that I relate to you in the first place.

14. We are in a process of evolving coherence. We should understand our place in the evolving universe, ourselves as thoughts in the mind of God with each of us living our

lives therefore within a cosmic context.

15. The old mechanical worldview could never succeed; it was flawed by its inability to explain or account for consciousness.

16. We can live as one universe, living in a reconciled and integrated way within our selves, others and the universe.

17. We are no longer separate; we live in a web of relationships; all is connected.

18. We have choices and responsibilities to care for ourselves, others, and our shared Global Home.

19. We are called to live in love and compassion not fear.

20. We realize that God is not in the sky, with a white beard, judging everyone, ready with his stick; God/the Divine/Other/the Unnameable/Mystery is part of our journey within and around us.

21. We are all equal; at the same time, we are all different. This diverse equality is to be respected and encouraged.

22. Spirituality is not privatized but social = praxis–informed theory, living theory.

23. Quantum science informs us of the physical and chemical truths of our lives here on earth.

24. Our soul sickness, despair, malaise, alienation, loneliness, hopelessness can be helped by taking on board the quantum realities – we belong!

25. Both oppressors and oppressed require radical change, transformation and metamorphosis from being ego-centred, fearful or self-complacent in our overwhelmed earth home which we share.

Quantum science and spirituality share the same purpose, the same vision, and the same message.

Chris Clarke, a UK physicist, wrote a paper titled, "Quantum Mechanics, Consciousness, and the Self", which I found helpful.

I have summarized some points below.

We have now escaped from the stranglehold of Cartesian dualism that led us to the story of a meaningless universe. Descartes described the separation and interaction between mind (thinking stuff) and matter (extended stuff) in terms of their having different functions and being different substances. Such a division as we have seen, is not viable.

The answer to "what is the world really like?" is a story that is as much about our selves as about the world, because in this picture we play a part in coordination with all other conscious beings and with the influence of the context of the entire universe, in shaping what the world is. We are co-creators in the universe – co-creators with God, if one chooses to use theistic terminology.

My consciousness will include within it aspects of all the other beings whom I perceive, and of people with whom I have an empathetic connection. We are not separated from each other and from the world as are the atoms in the Newtonian system, but are integrally connected with each other.

My choice arises from the whole of who I am, which has built up through the whole of my life. When I creatively move into a new way of seeing things, a new framework of meaning, then I am changing the way my consciousness is selecting within the histories in which I take part. This lies outside of the "mechanistic dynamics" and physics and goes to the core of the self. Ideas of value and responsibility flow from this source of creativity.

This picture affirms our humanity rather than denies it. This picture is consistent with existing science; no alternative New Age science needs to be invented. On the basis of this approach, we can reaffirm the values of our humanity and our connectivity with the world around us, while at the same time building on all we have learnt through the rigorous application of science. I believe only with this combination of the subjective dimension with established scientific knowledge will we find a future on this planet.

I also especially believe that this last sentence is crucial for us all to understand, embrace and appropriate within our own belief system and choices. I asked a friend: "Do you think that you try to live out your life with quantum spirituality?" Her response was:

"I think of quantum understanding as a web of everything – interrelationship and interconnection of all beings. I try to live open to and am open to synchronicity – a way of relating to whatever is in my world or energy to flow between myself and that sentient being. I believe in that oneness – we are only a part of the whole. The more synchronistic and present I am to self and other, then the energy happens – brings more joy, happiness, if I am more consciously aware of it. I don't understand the scientific terminology of it all – we all have a God box or word that draws us on further and further wanting to experience this connectedness, then the more we experience it the more joy, happiness and fulfilment we have in life.

"Not only do we experience synchronicity and connectedness; we become or are the rocks, sky, clouds and we have within us all the fullness of the universe as does each sentient being and that is what the connectedness is about. I am you and you are me.

"What creates blocks is when I fight with someone, even with a friend or someone across the world, I am fighting with my self–exploding atomic bombs on myself. Look at blocks to living this way of life because we can't connect otherwise.

"Mystics ask, what is the dross around the heart and soul that stops us living this way? I am happier if I am connected especially with the whole Universe and Communion of Saints with all that is available to us.

The whole sense of responsibility; I need to find ways to further my desire for compassion – the more we nurture it; it is the glue. Compassion is the filler of the web."

The search for a deeper understanding of living spirituality is growing mainly outside the "church", more in a development in partnership with the field of science. Science is moving at a quick pace as is our understanding of spirituality. We are part of a tidal wave for truth, freedom, concern, choice, responsibility and love.

We no longer embrace alienation and separation in our world. People are waking up: people are engaging in awareness raising and consciousness raising at so many levels for so many reasons – the Spirit is moving – are we ready?

By appropriating a deeper understanding of quantum science over the past fifteen years, I have grown in my understanding and knowledge in so many ways: spiritually, emotionally, intellectually and in all aspects of my life. There are more resources and more corporate and global growth in various areas of our lives. It is challenging me to keep abreast and make choices and decisions to change, to move out of my fixed and comfortable habits and to make what seems like risky leaps to a new way of knowing and being.

Are we listening to and seeing? ...
the voice of nature?

Chapter 6

Making the Change (to) Now

To help effect change, we have to change first. As our change helps change the world around us, we are also, in turn, changed more deeply. In this chapter, I will outline some understandings about how to change and how deep change and transformation is enabled.

It is easy enough to read a book like this and even to understand and embrace what is being outlined and suggested as a way of life. We can argue wholeheartedly with its importance and the essentialness of our part in this journey.

Yet, as we all know and experience, it seems like one thing to embrace such ideas and theories with every good intention to live them out. It is another thing however, to make the changes, even when we are thoroughly and utterly committed. We simply cannot seem to "walk our talk" as it were. Change is required, and we then realise that we don't know how to embrace it and allow it to happen.

This chapter will outline some pointers and descriptions suggested by various authors who are very learned in this field. There are accompanying websites to these teachings which allow you to continue study and learn further, if you so desire.

How to Change according to Spirituality Teachers
What is involved in our transformation and metamorphosis? With so many spiritual guides and theories, perhaps a different question is needed. How can we change? What is involved? Is there any agreement about what we need to do?

Some guides and recommendations do seem compatible. Yet others seem in direct opposition. Remember what one called the many "snake oil" opportunists, offering to help people who are floundering or seeking. People can end up confused, even traumatized in their search and efforts to find an authentic and healthy way forward.

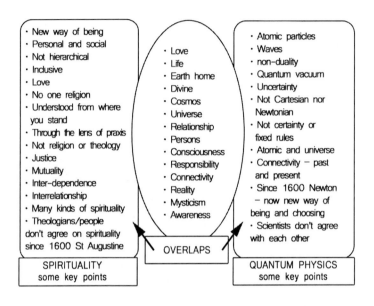

SPIRITUALITY — some key points:
- New way of being
- Personal and social
- Not hierarchical
- Inclusive
- Love
- No one religion
- Understood from where you stand
- Through the lens of praxis
- Not religion or theology
- Justice
- Mutuality
- Inter-dependence
- Interrelationship
- Many kinds of spirituality
- Theologians/people don't agree on spirituality since 1600 St Augustine

OVERLAPS:
- Love
- Life
- Earth home
- Divine
- Cosmos
- Universe
- Relationship
- Persons
- Consciousness
- Responsibility
- Connectivity
- Reality
- Mysticism
- Awareness

QUANTUM PHYSICS — some key points:
- Atomic particles
- Waves
- non-duality
- Quantum vacuum
- Uncertainty
- Not Cartesian nor Newtonian
- Not certainty or fixed rules
- Atomic and universe
- Connectivity – past and present
- Since 1600 Newton – now new way of being and choosing
- Scientists don't agree with each other

The graphic points to the overlaps of spirituality and quantum physics. A good guide will exhibit discernment, professionalism, experience, connectivity with others – both in oversight or supervisory roles as well as in requesting assistance or insights from others. The integration of what is on offer is also a clue as to how beneficial a guide might be. Otherwise we can end up compartmentalizing ourselves even more, trying to pull the various aspects of our lives together and getting even more confused in the attempt.

I have offered some input below, from people whose writing and perspectives have stood the test of time and authenticity and proven to be helpful. This is not by any means an exhaustive list but rather a starting point to consider what help and understanding is available from a variety of sources and perspectives, about "how to change". These are summaries of each guide's larger work and insight.

The Four Steps To Wisdom by Anthony de Mello, SJ

DeMello was a Jesuit from India who has written prolifically about change. I have included just a few points of his here.

1. The first thing you need to do is get in touch with negative feelings about which you may not even be aware.
2. Understand that the feeling is in you, not in reality. What spirituality is about is unlearning all the things taught at schools, but not taught how to live. Stop trying to change reality, trying to change the other person. We spend all our time and energy trying to change external circumstances. We don't have to change anything. The feeling is in you not in reality.
3. Never identify with that feeling. It has nothing to do with the "I". Don't define your essential self in terms of that feeling. You're defining yourself in terms of the feeling. That's your illusion; that's your mistake. What you need is to be free. What you need is to love. That's your nature.Wake up! You are not a puppet any longer, but now broken out of slavery and your prison... You don't have to do anything to acquire happiness. You don't have to do anything to be free. You drop something. Then you're free.
4. How do you change things? How do you change yourselves? The person who is asleep always thinks he/she'll feel better if somebody else changes. You're suffering because you are asleep, but you're thinking: "How wonderful life would be if somebody else would change; how wonderful life would be if my neighbour changed, my wife changed, my boss changed." (http://www.demello.org/articles/html)

When we change deeply, inside, it seems beyond our own doing. We change because we choose to take the time and become aware and to contemplate and embrace this new way of perceiving living this new vision.

Heather Eaton on Spiritual Awakening

Heather Eaton, who is a professor at St Paul's University, Ontario, Canada, offers insights on spiritual awakening.

She writes that we need a spiritual vision that teaches us how to be present to the earth, on earth's terms. She refers to Spirituality like breathing, as intimate and as vital as breath. It is about desire, a zest for life – the ability to feel awe and wonder, to experience reverence in the face of the immensity and elegance of existence.

Such awareness leads to a profound spiritual and moral awakening and to radical political actions. We need a deep ecological awakening – I don't know if less will be enough. To see and know the earth as such requires a new way of perceiving, and a confidence that to experience the earth as sacred is not quaint, irrelevant, heretical or idealistic.

To contemplate the earth – from the micro biotic and genetic levels to the dinosaurs, the processes and other life forms is a fantasy beyond human imagination. If we attend, even momentarily, to the dynamics of water, the inventiveness of birds, the ingenuity of insect communication and the emotions of mammals, then how is it possible not to be overwhelmed by the creativity, diversity, power and beauty?

Religions are about awakening to these deeper dimensions of reality. It is a spiritual imperative for our time. Religions have a crucial role to play in our era. Further, we cannot leave the public debates about religion and the ecological crisis in the hands of the right wing religious agenda. Not all religion is good religion. Superficial notions of religion or the reiteration of religious dogma will not suffice. Protectionist and imperialist stances prevent common efforts. Religions need to become self aware, and ecologically literate.

We need a vision that teaches us how to be present to the earth on earth's terms. If we can cultivate awareness of this magnificent earth and see ourselves as members of this earth community, then we will find spiritual resources that we have not yet imagined. *heaton@ustpaul.ca*; *http://tyne.ca/ief2007/node/18* . Eaton also offers three video presentations, which are to be found on the same web address.

Thomas Keating on "How to Change"

Father Keating practices, teaches and writes about "Centring Prayer and Meditation", which is a practice of meditation. He points out that as with all regular meditation practices it opens us up to our unconscious and deeper selves and allows our hidden pain and wounds to surface from the darkness of repression. Then follows the hard work and commitment to stay on the journey to wholeness as we learn to deal with what surfaces and so to be healed, so that we can be authentic, present and loving persons who no longer need to project our fears or live out our defences "on" others.

This work requires us to let go and let God/Divine/Other with our own continuing *yes* remaining active. It is a dynamic and necessary component of a mysterious relationship that surpasses all understanding.

In this process, we are emptied of the false gods to which we cling. It is not a linear journey but has overlapping nights of darkness as we participate in our own journey, intentionally furthering the process.

We cannot do it on our own. More grace is needed to be able to stay in the darkness of everything. It requires us to drop past conditioning and the control that society has over us – a control which has resulted in prejudices, projections, attachments and labels, to which we clutch. It is not about techniques but rather being a certain kind of person, that is who you become in your on-going journey.

We are *transformed* by the resonance of love. It is God who does the *transforming* – all we have to do is show up and start walking. We seek to become this transformed consciousness

that leads to an integrated sense of our whole being. The challenge is to come down from our rarefied atmosphere of the mountain of visions into the blood, sweat and tears of messy, daily struggle in the valley of tears, come from our heads to hearts and then to body, live our emotions and feelings and inhabit our bodies and let go of the pretence attached to our way of life. To be vulnerable is to become authentic.

If we come from honesty and the pursuit of justice in all orders of life while denouncing the status quo, our theological justice continues reflection in search for actions of transformation in society.

How do we transcend and transform the ego? How do we breathe life again into our lost true self to reach an appropriate maturity and responsible individuality? We must discern our egotism from our true self; we begin to do this by keeping a vigilant watch over the arrogance of self-righteousness of the ego.

Awareness and living in the present moment, with loving objective observing in the here and now, is the first and probably the last step to be taken in the journey towards spiritual freedom and light. The main work of transformation is to be transformed by the resonance of love, which is necessary to awaken to this self, which has the power of love to tame the false self and ego. What we most need is what we already are, our essential self; there is no escape; there is only coming home.

Father Laurence Freeman adds that the simple power of authentic practice, the daily doing of the work of being produces a conscious energy that pervades and instrumentalises all of our actions.

The art of the spiritual life is a fine balance between detachment and commitment; a dynamic equilibrium to balance exchange of energy and justice. *Meditation* changes our life because it teaches and trains us in the deep core of our being to a fundamental truth. Spiritual practice means taking the time for working at it; in this truth of poverty of spirit is the state of mind in which we grow and live the teaching and see how life exemplifies the teaching process of the spirit.

1. Detaching from the consumer mentality–spirituality is often degraded into more self-help or forms of cultural narcissism.
2. Detachment from our attachment to vices – self-centeredness and patterns of the mind that support them require the force of detachment before they can be loosened and begin to change.
3. Letting go of attachment – material and mental.
4. The work in-between requires our dedicated integration of detachment and commitment – letting go and keeping on.
5. Spiritual authenticity bestows personal authority, an authority of compassion that places gentleness above force, insight above condemnation and healing above division. It is the authority of love that becomes embodied in the human heart of every person of good will.

Liberating oneself from inner compulsions and committing to the service of others – this certainly is hard work. Doing anything that transcends our own personal benefit and serves a wider world is difficult. This is not the work of a month or a year, but the road that leads to life.

Desire is the key in the spiritual life and is the mainspring of growth while trusting in Divine help to affect the transformation in us that this other desires, in partnership. Meditation coupled with mindfulness practice throughout the day attacks the three energy centres of the false self in several ways.

So, to summarize:

1. Resting in God – doors to the subconscious go ajar and some of what was held in it slips through to consciousness. Meditation seems a critical function of exposing and bringing to awareness the false self's *strategies and wounds* that necessitated their development.
2. We can then choose to act on the impulse or to give it expression or not.
3. We come with an open and surrendered heart therefore opening doors to the Divine's transforming grace.

Additional Considerations for Our Journey

Here I would like to add my own summary of spiritual growth. All human growth and spiritual growth are linked. As we journey to love, truth and meaning, we encounter what we often call blocks, brick walls, dark places, no-go areas; we want to stop and hide or run away.

Often we do run away in effect, resorting to alcohol, drugs, or other forms of avoidance to try to calm our anxieties and growing fears of our inability to weather the storms and grow, to find light instead of darkness. We are overwhelmed and sinking and so seek respite in whatever way we can. We affect ourselves but also others on their own journeys with all of our choices. The picture is complex and compounded.

It can feel like a vicious circle with no way out. We feel out of control and at the mercy of everything and everyone else. We feel powerless, even oppressed and long to be able to crawl out from under all that weighs us down. It is at these particular times of shock, despair, darkness, confusion, terror and the like that there can be deeper growth, change and transformation.

We are all on our journeys. They are all individual and

separate and yet they are connected. There are some points of contact and similarities; we can learn from the experience of others. Over many centuries, people have written prolifically. There is a wealth of wisdom from which we can learn; true learning is a challenge and a change, which require us, at times, to unlearn and to relearn.

What do we need? Whom do we believe? How do we know? How does that make any difference to our experience and way forward? What really helps – practically – what tools, what various theories? There may be lots of books, words, ideas, and theories that people share with us. Yet, when we are floundering, how can we make sense of it all?

Others can help us as we journey together. Those who have experienced something similar on their own journeys are those who are worthy and experienced in these matters. We can tell who they are by the fruits of their lives – if they too live in love with compassion and not with power over others but living in power "with" us.

We all continually have to choose – to grow in *conscious awareness* – into consciousness or not. This process of change is not linear, head, intellectual or rational; it is not top down. A process is a process – and the journey is more important than the end result. Thus, process is our life journey.

Our process is on-going – moment-by-moment and filled with choices taking place in our bodies, minds and spirits. This path involves us taking responsibility as active players in our own journey and process. We are not like puppets on a string, living with no choice, living out a blueprint but we can choose.

We can unlearn and re-learn as individuals and as groups, depending on our commitment to transformation and change. We can become aware and change on many levels as individuals, family, partnerships, relationships, groups, businesses, churches, societies.

Vanessa Parffrey's "Nine Way Markers (for Leadership)"

Our journeys are not only personal but also take place at group, organizational and global levels. We all affect each other. Parffrey helps us to consider the group aspect through what she refers to as "Way Markers".

The journey metaphor is of travelling, with a group, reminding people to keep hearts and minds on the overall goal. She quotes T.S. Elliott "in order to arrive at what you do not know ... you must go by the way of ignorance". Leadership of the Spirit is not a linear activity nor are you certain you will arrive since the climate might change, resources run out, more interesting paths might appear but as you lead the journey the rest will follow and the end result is the by-product of the process" with the process as the task and way to get results, with flat structures, process and relationship being valued over product.

So the journey is not about arriving at the end of a linear road but about revisiting old and known situations so you are back where you started but seeing it with new eyes. Therefore the reflective or experiential learning cycle is important with its four stages:

(a) experience,
(b) reflective observation,
(c) conceptualization (making sense); and
(d) doing (including forming plans).

Then we can end up back at the beginning but in a different place, in a spiral of change. Parffrey cautions about doing a mini-loop by starting at the doing, which prompts experiences and leads to forming and re-formulating plans. This short-circuit takes little time for reflection or making sense. Effective movement can only take place when all four elements are undertaken in the specified order.

We don't then continue in the same vicious circle going round and round the same route, never moving on. We need time alone to think and take stock, discuss and reflect with others and engage with others' viewpoints in literature and discussion.

Personal spiritual growth and development can be seen as a pilgrimage in an on-going open-ended journey, where we need to trust the process/journey and "reflective practice" can be helpful. In all spiritual development, time set aside to be alone, to be quiet, to think, pray and just be is "key" for lasting growth of knowledge and wisdom which is difficult to achieve. Otherwise, we are left instead with cosmetic change instead of getting in touch with our own wisdom.

Community

The journey is not only individual but often also with communities of people moving on together, working together towards common aims, as groups of learners on the same exploratory and transformative journey. Collaboration is necessary – not "apparent collaboration" with each still doing their own thing and competing. A good model is honeybees working together co-operatively, mutually inter-dependent with a common purpose with clearly defined roles. Spiritual development is by way of community, with reflective learning and discernment done "with" others, with the total community and not just a select few.

Vision

It is much better to spend time building a common set of ideas and purposes than to rush to bring the individual leader's plans to fruition. Therefore leaders need to communicate their vision, perhaps using the language of the spirit, where symbolism, icons, poetry and music are used to express what words cannot easily do. There is more to life than meets the eye: experiencing awe and wonder, beauty and mystery, with educators first becoming mystics to recover their own potential for contemplation, wonder and stillness, a relationship to the natural world and a thirst for learning.

Values

Parffrey found that through the very process of exploring values a community is formed rather than living out the prevailing management ethos which is "done to others" as in "social engineering", where people are manipulated with sanctions and rewards. Setting budgets and priorities are determined by different values, beliefs, ideologies and purposes. Therefore a leader needs to be in touch with their own value base and then set a climate in which common understandings can be articulated, creating opportunities for shared meaning.

Just "stating" the conditions needed to bring about improvement isn't enough because there is a relationship between change and ethics since change is a moral issue – "towards what are we changing, for what purpose, to what ends and by what means, whose agenda are we following and who is calling the tune and paying the piper?" The total integration of the personal and collective allows people to lead with integrity; anything less is just sophisticated social engineering.

Integrity

Covey describes integrity as "honestly matching works and feelings with thoughts and actions with no desire other than for the good of others, without malice or desire to deceive, take advantage or manipulating or control, constantly reviewing your intent as you strive for congruence." Otherwise we cannot be trustworthy. It is change in ourselves, not in the system or others around us; then we stop blaming others, because the only place we can be sure of ever bringing about change is in our own hearts. Leaders cannot cause anyone to "do" anything; they can only create the conditions in which others can learn and grow, leaving them free to journey or not, to be or not to be. Spiritual companionship means walking with another, providing the conditions that will enable the other, creating a climate of growth but leaving the actual walking to the other.

Relationship

Leadership is about relationships and concern for the entire well-being of the organization or community with ability to improve and change which happens through interpersonal relationship, since the path is one undertaken in and through relationship, founded on our individual relationship with the Divine, which is developed and lived out with others. Our journey is made sense of in relationship to others, since as human beings we are in relationship and connected to others and the rest of creation. Human relationships are at the heart of all world religions, concerned with the basic dilemma: how we can live fully true to ourselves and also live in community with others as social responsible beings.

Love

Love is the hardest emotion or word with which to deal. Parffrey traces the notions of love in theology and the secular world of educational psychology. Carl Rogers stated that respect, genuineness, empathy are the three interpersonal qualities for growth and learning in relationships, where we don't hide behind masks or power, condemning or putting down others. Empathy is when we walk and feel with the other, without power or personal agenda. Nourishment helps provide self-esteem, dignity, collaboration and motivation.

Risk

Risk-taker leaders are able to walk alongside others, listen, nurture, encourage, hold the vision, and protect the values of the community. If the organisation is functioning as a beehive, it will have interdependency and mutuality. She believes that organisations need to devise a "process" which underpins standard-raising activities.

Changing our thinking/theories/understanding/learning

So what does all of this have to do with quantum physics? Here I want to provide a summary of the basic principles of quantum physics. Then I hope to build on it as a way of changing our thinking, theories, understanding and learning. As we are able to embrace this popular and growing expanding understanding of quantum physics and its relevance to the totality of our lives, we can more relevantly and excitedly embrace the theory, which then in turn, affects our practice, and so we have praxis. Learning about quantum physics requires both deep learning and considered effort. It does require a huge *shift* – a quantum shift – before we can choose whether to embrace and explore it further or not. We always *choose* how we live.

Yet, the quantum shift is more than thinking good thoughts from some happy psychology. It rests on the science of quantum physics which we have introduced. Here we dig deeper in order to understand spirituality in a different way.

German physicists Max Planck and Albert Einstein got the ball rolling when breaking apart atoms. Planck determined, while studying light as discrete packets called photons, that the energy of a photon is its frequency of vibration times a constant (which he named the Planck constant). Einstein noted that this made light a particle of energy. This clashed with the agreed understanding that light is a wave, much like seawater washing upon a shore. Erwin Schrödinger (a German trained Austrian) compared wave and energy equations, and all were surprised when the two were the same. Then Niels Bohr (a Danish physicist) showed that light was neither wave nor particle until it was measured. In short, when you change the way you look at things, you change the things you are looking at.

Atoms interact with one another by exchanging or entangling

photons. Once they have become entangled, forever afterward a change in one atom influences the other because of a sort of subatomic exchange between the two atoms. What is termed *the zero point field* (and its equations) aggregates into a single field of all particles, all matter.

The five main theses of quantum theory are (Baksa, 2011):

1. Energy is not continuous, but comes in small but discrete units, or quanta.
2. The elementary particles behave both like particles and like waves.
3. The movement of these particles is inherently random.
4. It is physically impossible to know both the position and the momentum of a particle at the same time. The more precisely one is known, the less precise the measurement of the other is.
5. Particles can influence one another no matter how far apart they are separated.

How does this relate to spirituality? Well, to put it simply, we are all one. The stars, galaxies, creatures, and whatever else–we are together. We also influence each other as well as all of reality.

Zohar states that the spiritual vacuum many live in results in individual freedom, but not in any commitment to a shared social reality. Relationships are important. Seeing our purposes and ourselves fully as part of the universe provides us with a coherent world picture–one that includes ourselves.

Yet achieving commitment to a shared social reality is not something to be attained so much as recognized. Conscious human beings share some of our conscious nature with all other conscious creatures. The quantum field theory proposes the link between the physics of human consciousness and the physics of the quantum vacuum, which is the basic, fundamental under-lying reality of which everything in this universe, including ourselves is a part. It is like a "bubbling soup" or a theory of everything.

Quantum physics gives a physical basis to a more holistic, less fragmented way of looking at ourselves; the whole world of creation shares a physics with everything else in the universe, with human bodies, all other living creatures, the coherent grounds state, matter and relationship, and the quantum vacuum itself.

Because we are all one, an understanding of spirituality is one not of privatised spirituality but rather one of justice, which integrates inner and outer ethics. There is an accompanying need to move from the Dominant Mechanistic Paradigm to the Inclusive and Spiritual Paradigm. More research is needed from educators, spiritual guides and spiritual directors so that we are not simply living out our "ego" *translatively*, as Wilber cautions. He says we must live in the reality in which we are all connected, as part of each other as quantum physics indicates, within our relationships, organisations and world. (Wilber, 1997)

A human being is a tiny microcosm of a cosmic being – we are made of the same stuff and held together by the same dynamics as everything else in the universe. Relational holism is the essence of consciousness. There is a dynamic on-going dialogue between past and present, forming a new quantum self.

Quantum self is a more fluid self, changing and evolving at every moment. The "I" and "we" is "both/and" in the new physics of consciousness. "You" and "I" become "we". There is a physical basis for interpersonal relationship; woven into the fabric of our soul are all the intimate relationships we have ever had, where neither individuality nor relationship is lost.

Each of us carries within both aspects of our own past and the aspects of the pasts of those with whom we are in an intimate relationship. So we have a bond with those who have gone before, we are (in part) them; aspects of their being are inter-woven into my own. Their past is part of my own living life.

Who I am now arises from a tapestry of interwoven patterns in the quantum system of my brains and am I-and-you, within time and beyond. With the quantum view, we understand the extent to which we are all physically interwoven, and this requires a revolution in our whole way of perceiving ourselves and our relations to others. This also helps us to transcend the poverty of our lives as formulated by reason... living our lives within a cosmic context.

Human consciousness and the whole world of its creation share a physics with everything else in this universe, with the human body, with all other living things and creatures. The quantum world transcends dichotomy between individual and relationship within a context, stressing dynamic relationship as the basis of all that is. When fully transformed we can be responsible and be able to have a generative influence on spirituality today.

Commitment is important and it takes energy to keep making decisions to keep in relationship with another. I am my relationships – we can choose to embrace these insights or not. To the extent that we do is the extent to which we will benefit ourselves and all those with whom we are in contact, which now is understood to mean everyone and everything. Or we may prefer instead to be lazy.

We can live our quantum relationships and spirituality together

The poverty of meaning in our lives today is formulated by reason. But in our awakening resistance to oppression, we can transform relationships in society through revitalizing spiritual energy, empowering a transformative praxis. All who are oppressed can be empowered.

Through integrating science/physical and theological-spiritual realities, we realise the need to change existing imbalanced and dysfunctional relationships, models and structures, so we can live in connected relationships in a transformed society of mutuality. We realise the extent to which we are physically inter-woven and this affects our way of being in the world and our understanding of our relationship to ourselves, others, the Divine and the earth.

With the basic physics of matter and relationship and with the coherent ground of the quantum vacuum itself, it becomes impossible to imagine a single aspect of our lives that is not drawn into one coherent whole. Since every particle in the universe can be related to every other particle a quality of unbroken wholeness is created. The quantum self is a more fluid self, changing and evolving at every moment.

There is no space between objects; therefore there are no separate objects – "separate" has no foundation in reality. An essential definition of consciousness is of relationship and the mind-body duality in humans is a reflection of wave-particle duality that underlies all that is. In this way, a human being is a tiny microcosm of cosmic being. We are made of the same stuff and held together by the same dynamics as everything else in the universe and vice versa.

I have made a summary list of points below which helps us to make sense of what quantum physics means and what living it out and its application within our lives can actually mean as well. This list serves as a reminder because for us truly to embrace a transformative praxis we have to know and under-stand it deeply and be willing to do the very hard work of remembering, becoming more aware and choosing to change. That is how our conscious awareness changes – with the hard work of consciously choosing to remember and consciously apply those changes.

This has to happen over and over again. It also helps if we are linked with others who are thinking and living similarly so we are not so isolated and we can also remind each other of these pointers and reality on our journeys.

Important points drawn from quantum physics are:

1. Quantum physics gives us a physical basis for connectivity – for us to move from "I" to "We". We can therefore have more stable relationships.
2. Quantum physics points out that we need to make a choice and commitment in our consciousness to relate to all beings in our world as family.
3. We live in a web of relationships – intricately connected.
4. If we do not understand quantum physics and take it on board, we are missing a lot and will continue to want quick fixes and stay the same, unchanged, isolated, separate, spiritually numb and dumb.
5. Moving from a Newtonian physics of rationalism with its "objective" study of separate matter to now understanding Quantum Physics which recognizes that particles and waves are connected, brings about a holistic understanding that there is an integration of logic with senses and feelings which are more holistic.
    It can include mystic /spirituality as well as body; no longer dualistic.
6. Most scientists can't make this move and continue to research at subatomic levels with new findings which for them have no application to human life, spiritual life and consideration for the betterment of the world. This furthers the control of life and nature in non-holistic ways.
7. Quantum Physics looks at subatomic as well as the cosmos which deals with uncertainty.
    Therefore:
    Nature is no longer seen as "other";
    lives are not formulated by reason;
    there is a seamless whole and a non-fragmented world.
8. We have lost contact with bodies and lived in our heads

but now we don't have to – there was no other knowledge but "scientific knowledge"! It was Newtonian reason believing that atoms and particles of light had somehow simply fallen into place by accident to compose the world in which we live.

9. *Holistic science* looks at science in the context of society, cultures and spirit recognizing that we exist in a web of relationships rather than in isolation. The understanding then is that *research has to be done in context.*

10. Scientists can then consider and think about the effect of their science on environment, community, culture and spirituality and the psyche of human beings – "soil, soul, society".

11. Quantum Physics studies very large and very small things and studies matter and how it interacts – describing the universe around us and predicting how the universe will behave – the stars, planets, galaxies and small pieces of matter – atoms, electrons, sound, light and other waves, energy, heat and radioactivity and time and space – atomic physics, nuclear physics and particle physics.

12. The Quantum vacuum is a sea of energy underlying all reality in which particles come spontaneously and then vanish and dissolve quietly back into the vacuum, which is a sea of fluctuating energy.

13. Matter – mind/souls were separated in Newtonian/ Cartesian physics.

14. Still contemporary quantum physics needs to recognise spirit, psyche and consciousness; we no longer have to choose between body and soul. Quantum Physics opens up deeper connectedness constituting a much richer web of relationships reaching beyond time and space in the wider universe.

15. Newtonian understanding in the 1600's believed that it

was either a wave OR a particle not both/and.

16. The ability to describe reality in the form of waves is at the heart of Quantum Physics. The atomic world is different than our world. Belief in the independent existence of things leads to various ideologies that tend to divide humanity: racism, extreme nationalism and Marxist class struggle. This tendency to perceive things as inherently divided and disconnected leads us to believe that divisions are essentially independent and self-existent.

"Quantum", in Latin, means 'how great'or 'how much'. Science is dealing with the amount of energy of an atom at rest (a discrete unit that quantum theory assigns to certain physical quantities.) It is the underlying mathematical framework of many fields of all physics and chemistry.

Quantum mechanics explains many features of our world, for example, the laser, transistor, microchip, electron, microscopy, magnetic resonance imaging. (Wikipedia) The explanation for connectivity comes through the idea of the *quantum state* of the particles implicated in our sense of awareness, which is a structure beyond time and space and equals a sense of meaningfulness from the direct connection we have with the wider universe.

Implications of Quantum Physics for living out our spirituality – appropriation

a. It gives us a PHYSICAL basis for understanding that we are not separate, as people, as individuals with egos only, but that we are essentially and atomically connected with our past, present and future, with others, our Gaia, living world, the Divine Other and our galaxy.

b. We can get involved, not stay depressed, numb and spiritually dumb, isolated and separate and disillusioned, but can join the journey of the few who are becoming conscious, waking up and becoming aware and taking responsibility for genuine loving, caring and change. We can take political responsibility and help the 80 per cent of the world who remain oppressed, even by Quantum Physics which is under the thumb of the establishment with money for research as the driving and determining force even in universities.

c. We do not have to be in collusion with the 'systems' because we *know* that there is a *physical basis* and reality; SCIENCE now also says that we are connected. We can have a voice and emphasize that at every level of our lives, in personal, family, church, social, national, organisational and patriarchal systems.

d. We can see a way out with this new reality of Quantum Physics yet to be employed and spoken out and owned by many, holistically embracing the spiritual, feeling, experiential, sensorial side of life (feminine) despite money, threat or oppression of scientists.

e. The implication for authentic and true spirituality then is that we each personally have to take the transformational journey of change and ownership from old Theology and old Science to the new spirituality and Quantum Physics, to be able to live inclusively, non-prejudiced, and to be able to throw off the old conditioning which we have subscribed to even unconsciously, and then RISK – CARE – BELONG. With others we can be harbingers and join even more people to see if there can be enough of us joined in the web of connectedness to make a global change before it is too late for us all.

f. It is a huge task and challenge, both from the SPIRITU- ALITY and from the QUANTUM PHYSICS under- standings, put together one complementing the other, with the joint message of no separation, alienation, isolation but rather 'together' taking responsibility to really love and care. It is a long, hard, sacrificial and costly journey, not easy, not a quick-fix, not a theory or theology or dogma or just intellectual assent only. RATHER it is a 'living theory' and a 'living spirituality' with the help of the Spirit, realizing that with grace we can live a life of mutual empowerment, where we are ALL equal and connected and so do unto others as we would do unto ourselves. HOWEVER we can only love others to the extent that we can love ourselves; if we do not love ourselves we just continue the pattern of destructive, unloving practice which leads to defence, fear, war and lack of trust and belief in anything other than ourselves. It requires and leads to intercultural co-existence and co-operation.

g. When we realize the urgency of planetary breakdown and various crises, catastrophes, we can intervene. It's our choice! With a significant number of people as a critical mass in society, a fundamental and radical *transformation* can be triggered in our globally, interconnected society thus leading to the dignity of all cultures and all people being respected.

Understanding the world as a whole system to be maintained with individual, collective, social, economic, political and cultural responsibility, we can help lead it to growth into a peaceful, co-operative human family. We also then need to grow spiritually and emotionally, equally. (Laszlo)

h. Spirituality is already well understood through Quantum Physics. If also embraced by theology and religion, it could bring people back into a 'community' of authentic, healthy, non-patriarchal institutions of shared mutuality and relational power.

People having "inner" and/or "outer" spirituality searches on their own or alone can be very risky indeed because on their spiritual explorations they are vulnerable to all sorts of people who are self-styled spiritual gurus and as Higgins wrote "snake oil entrepreneurs".

Quantum Science recognises that the whole is greater than the parts. We become more aware of global consciousness and our earth home through contemplation and can then be co-creative with the entire creation, and come home to ourselves to love and be loved, to love others and ourselves. (O'Murchu 2004)

Irvin Laszlo – The *Quantum Shift in the Global Brain*

Laszlo has been described by Grof as the world's greatest systems theorist, interdisciplinary scientist and philosopher. He has written 83 books.

Laszlo also emphasizes and therefore underlines much of what has already been written. He refers to our global crisis believing that the global climate is at a tipping point and so there is a need for transformation within our fragmented civilization so that we can all live in a peaceful and co-operative society, living in solidarity.

He re-iterates that we all have a choice, and if we shift together as a society we can tip the scales at business, economically, culturally, politically, culturally and socially at regional and global levels, that is individually and collectively working together.

Laszlo believes that deep religious and spiritual experience and meditation is conducive to our inner growth. We can achieve coherence even across time and space if we go beyond our ego bound limited consciousness. We will then have an empathy with people, cultures, animals and plants.

This change requires respect for each other's differences, beliefs and life styles, recognizing equal value and dignity in a diverse intercommunicating world.

Miriam Therese Winters – *Paradoxology* – *Spirituality in a Quantum Universe*

Winters is a Medical Missionary Sister and is a professor of liturgy, worship and spirituality at Hartford Seminary, Connecticut. She has written 15 books.

She emphasizes solutions similar to what others have previously referred. I include her voice since she is another who suggests a possible way forward. She uses different words but they are stating the same message, it seems.

She suggests that we immerse ourselves in all quantum energy around us and within us, even seeing the Spirit as that primal energy's source. Winters notes that both science and spirituality surpass understanding and can only be recognized by their fruits – such as wisdom and mystery which are not the results of logical conclusions. Our imagination is helpful to see new vision and new vistas.

Spirituality can contribute to conversations about quantum perspectives since it can set certainties aside. She suggests that spirituality and Physics take the next stage together since the wisdom of our separate disciplines is incomplete. Genuine quantum spirituality doesn't envisage the Divine as apart from us but rather everywhere, permeating the world, in the world, with the world in the Divine.

A quantum leap and a leap of faith are similar since spirituality can live in peace with questions and ambiguity. We have created our world's problems and crisis and so we too can change it if we choose.

Zohar, Laszlo, and Winters are giving similar perspectives, understandings, and insights. I find it important to read, re-read, listen, hear and understand these visionaries. There are many others, of course. Many of us are still stuck or partially stuck in our old ways of thinking and being, true to the way we were taught as children or adults, with the various systems or institutions of which we were or are still a part of. Those perspectives may be archaic or stuck in an old rut, not keeping up with the obvious events and situations in which we all find ourselves within our global home.

Part Three

Bread Crumbs for the Journey

Chapter 7

Fruits and Consequences of Growth

In the previous chapter, we explored our isolated, narrow lives with our restrictive perspectives. We are almost unaware of the great crisis the whole world and we are facing. Our earth home is dying and so are we with it. Many scientists say we have ten years or maybe less to turn things around before it is too late.

We now know the fruit; we can stop projecting our need for dominance of others and our world. We unpack what the word *authority* means as that which sets us free to be in communion with others and all. There is no spiritual elitism; we are all members of life journeying together along the path. We can join the path with those who have gone before us on this journey.

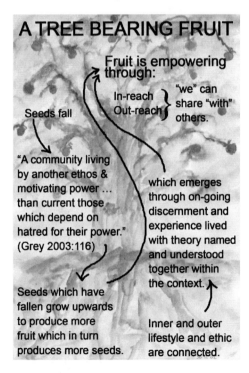

A TREE BEARING FRUIT

Fruit is empowering through:

In-reach
Out-reach
} "we" can share "with" others.

Seeds fall

"A community living by another ethos & motivating power ... than current those which depend on hatred for their power." (Grey 2003:116)

which emerges through on-going discernment and experience lived with theory named and understood together within the context.

Seeds which have fallen grow upwards to produce more fruit which in turn produces more seeds.

Inner and outer lifestyle and ethic are connected.

Fruit of Such Changes

The main fruits are that:

1. Discrimination, disadvantage, domination and oppression can be replaced by empowerment and enabling.
2. The test of the morality of an action will be the degree to which it promotes growth of the spirit.
3. The degree of enlightenment is the intensity of the light of truth and love in the life of each person – how they pronounce sensitively with compassion and wisdom on moral questions that so deeply affect the self-identity and feelings of others.

KEY HALLMARKS ARE

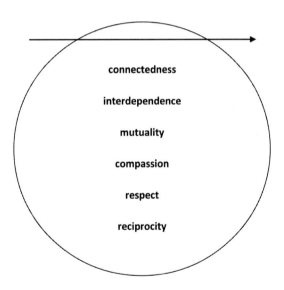

connectedness

interdependence

mutuality

compassion

respect

reciprocity

The hope and belief of many who are involved in the field of spirituality rests on the ideas that:

1. When enough individuals and organisations shift to the

new paradigm, there is greater likelihood that society will transform as well. (Neal et al, 2000:5-14)

2. Small pockets of people who can humbly advocate a "true integral spirituality" by example and liberation are those who have experienced a radical and "authentic transformation" at the deepest seat of consciousness itself. (Wilber, 1997)

3. Living more than a superficial change, *Teilhard de Chardin* believed that spirit is ultimate reality and a spiritual outlook is the only authentic outlook; all life, at the human level, is 'spiritual life' or it is, quite literally meaningless.

Each of us is a spiritual being, which makes communication between me and another human being something more than the mere interaction of sound waves and so forth. When he talked about the phenomenon of *spirit*, "physically defined by a certain tension of consciousness on the surface of the earth", he wrote:

Theoretically,
this transformation of love is quite possible.
What paralyzes life is failure to believe
and failure to dare.
The day will come when,
after harnessing space,
the winds,
the tides,
and gravitation,
we shall harness for God the energies of love.
And on that day, for the second time
In the history of the world,
we shall have discovered fire. (Gallagher, 1988)

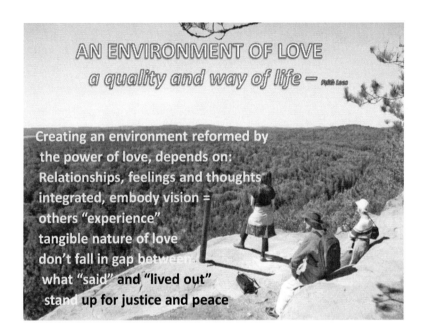

AN ENVIRONMENT OF LOVE
a quality and way of life — Faith Levi

Creating an environment reformed by
the power of love, depends on:
Relationships, feelings and thoughts
integrated, embody vision =
others "experience"
tangible nature of love
don't fall in gap between
what "said" and "lived out"
stand up for justice and peace

Chapter 8

Spotting Spoiled Fruit

We can now begin to recognise what we have been "learning" about what spirituality is. It is also *recognised*; that is, studying spirituality is deeply transformative and life changing for those who study it. It *cannot* help but be such, and therefore pastoral help and learning is often built into course programmes. It would also be a need for all who immerse themselves in becoming more aware of what spirituality means for them. There are many implications resulting from the deep learning and experience involved. It is not just rational, intellectual and theoretical but every aspect of our lives are implicated and involved in change.

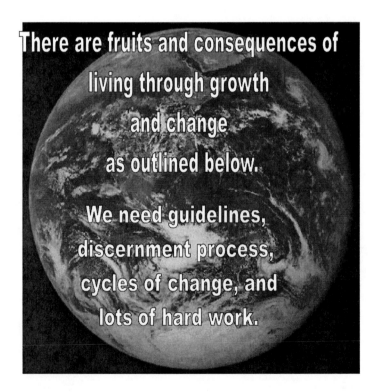

There are fruits and consequences of living through growth and change as outlined below.

We need guidelines, discernment process, cycles of change, and lots of hard work.

This chapter helps us to see the various guidelines which can be helpful in times of change, growth and transformation, as we move from either having been oppressors or victims in any aspects of our lives; that is as we move to live in the circle of mutuality with healthy relationships and structures.

Our problems are all interconnected and so collaboration within our global home seems essential in order to find interconnected solutions. There is both a need for caution as well as for some sort of common opinion and understanding since we are all confronted with our global, ecological, spiritual and social crises, which are also accompanied by a wave of interest in spirituality as we seek to grapple with the deepest yearnings in our hearts.

The key words which emerged from the references included in previous chapters, can give us a sense of some of the difficulties and concerns in understanding contemporary spirituality. They are: competing and conflicting, foreign, purveyors of dubious wares, not a quick-fix, challenges easy spiritualities, misunderstanding, dubious claims, secularised and psychologised spirituality, dumb culture, spiritually ill, smorgasbord, taboo subject, politics, ecology, socio-economics, embodied in individuals, groups and organisations, accountability, patriarchal consciousness, interconnected, transformation, global justice and responsibility, compassion. Therefore it is easy to understand the present and on-going need for transformational action-orientated spirituality, a spirituality of collaboration, global spirituality, holistic spirituality, spiritual democracy, ecumenical spirituality and spirituality of organisational renewal, all within an "environment of love".

"Connected knowing" is seeking to understand from within (Reason and Bradbury 2001:11). Our "embodied knowing" means that we first have to learn with our "selves" in an on-going way, with our own bodies, minds and souls, appreciating that wholeness was not linear perfection and that the living out of "spirituality" included an interdependence with the self, others, the earth and sacred, not an individualistic activity. Instead as we have seen, it encompassed political, social, ecological and interpersonal concerns, "with" others, with a "bottom-up theory". The more we learn the more our "practice" is improved.

We now "understand" what Au writes, that *Holistic Spirituality* links with every aspect of human development: psychological, spiritual, interpersonal and political lives, viewing spirituality as a particular way of being in the world, concerned with helping people to embody in a life-style the values they profess verbally. Thus it entails choices and decisions about the way we spend our time, money and resources, and issues around work, leisure, prayer, politics, sex and relationships.

Holistic spirituality attempts to find an outlook that will integrate people's lives sufficiently to give a sense of increasing wholeness and guide them in fashioning a concrete way of living out their spirituality. Enabling people to forge a more vital link between faith and daily life, a holistic approach to the spiritual life helps to heal the dichotomies and divisions that have forced so many to be schizophrenic in living out religious beliefs, and helps to overcome this pernicious schizophrenia between soul, body, brain and heart and thus become whole. (Au, 1993: 488-491)

There are often political and financial consequences and costs to our increased spiritual awareness. It requires a big paradigm shift from understanding our spiritual lives in individualistic terms towards one that embraces a wider reality, which is fundamental to authentic spirituality as O'Murchu pointed out. He stated that unless we are right in our relationships with other creatures, the planet and the Cosmos, we cannot be right with the Divine.

Spirituality is about living out the totality of life, not in compartments or just in our thoughts or ideologies/theologies but in an embodied and connected way with justice, care and love; it is social and political since we are all part of each other.

If our understanding is transformative, then we also experience an entry into the full breadth and depth of the human and cosmic journey in all its realms: the psychological, social, cultural, political, economic, ecological, and cosmological evolution and history of our world as we travel through this world as human persons. Our personal and communal spiritual journeys involve a commitment to the betterment of creation helping to bring about justice. (Byrne, 1993:565-577)

For many, the spiritual search happens "outside of the sanctuary" of the institutionalised church or organised religion but as we have read spirituality has a wide berth today. Having enough "room for all" is a great challenge for some in their search for an authentic spirituality praxis, that is how to welcome and interface with people from other faiths, religions, New Age, agnostics, atheists or pagans. "Equal opportunity" means trying to combat discrimination, imbalances and injustices, under representation or exclusion in order to get rid of discriminatory barriers, tackling underlying reasons why some groups are not promoted. To be effective diversity must make a difference by offering people more opportunities to fulfil their potential and in so doing radically alter the institution that previously excluded them.(Younge, 2002) That is what spirituality practice is about.

A "successful worldview must draw in levels of the personal, social and spiritual into one coherent whole so the world will not fragment and the success or failure rests ultimately with the individual ... with the understanding that the extent to which we are physically interwoven requires a revolution in our whole way of perceiving ourselves and our relation with others". (Zohar, 1991:216,133-134)

To try to embrace and live out an authentic spirituality requires us to move beyond personal terms toward one that embraces our wider global reality. "Spirituality" is complex because it affects us all personally and in our relationships with self, others, the Other and our earth so we can authentically play our part in our global home.

DISCRIMINATION, DISADVANTAGE, DOMINATION, OPPRESSION

REPLACED BY EMPOWERMENT AND ENABLING

As we live our life journey with all its various cycles

It seems that people *are* trying to live out a life of spirituality when they begin to realise that it includes both personal and social considerations:

1. an empowering and relational quality of life,
2. an effort to correct imbalances in relationship to others, the Sacred and our earth home,
3. an embracing of justice and empowerment "with" others
4. a choice to deal with real issues, responsibilities and conditions
5. a realization that spirituality is embodied – as a particular way of "being in the world".
6. a presentation particularly of a new worldview of mutuality
a) where the personal, social and spiritual are one coherent whole,
b) where *all* aspects of life and decisions are included – not separating out the sacred and the secular, nor the

individual and the social.

7. Spirituality is

a) not just a theory and ideology but rather living with "felt knowing" and experience,

b) not just individually but systemically and in their contexts.

8. Spirituality is embodied in people

a) in their structures, attitudes, ethos, relationships, context, vision, mission and practice

b) through their life structure, life style, and professed values, trying to integrate body, mind and spirit

9. Spirituality is lived out

a) within an empowering and enabling environment where justice and peace can be lived

b) in actual relationships – not understood in "individual terms"

The life and health of individuals, groups, organisations and society is fundamental to healthy praxis.

10. "Living spirituality" happens when people "are" what they are talking about:

a) Living *with* not over or under people who are thus enabled and empowered. Others can tell by the fruit.

b) Love overcomes a "praxis of exclusion" when we stop discriminating and exclude noone.

c) Love involves "deep democracy" with socio-political awareness and entails choices and decisions in all aspects of life.

11. Spirituality doesn't discriminate *contexts*

a) in its passion for democratic, right, and interactive relationships in a libratory, emancipatory, empowering and enabling environment.

b) Love of God and neighbour are inseparable

12. Spirituality links all aspects of our lives

a) psychological,

b) spiritual,

c) interpersonal and

d) political.

13. Spirituality is transformational–healing divisions, dualism and dichotomies.

14. We are all confronted with our global, ecological, spiritual and social crises.

15. Connected knowing grows from

a) understanding from within, learning from within our bodies, minds and souls,

b) letting go of outdated ideas to which we cling.

Most people still work with the old dualistic models; in evolutionary spirituality we need a whole integral picture.

16. Living out spirituality

a) includes interdependence with self, others, the earth and the sacred

b) is not individualistic activity but encompasses political, social, ecological and interpersonal concerns "with" others

c) is a particular way of being in the world

17. "Living spirituality" entails choices and decisions about how we spend time, money and resources

a) Social, political and financial consequences cannot be right with God unless right in relation to others, creatures, planet and cosmos

b) It requires a big paradigm shift from understanding the spiritual life in individualistic terms to one which embraces a wider reality

18. In not living life in compartments, in ideology/theology but in an embodied and connected way with justice, care and love, we are all physically interwoven.

19. Inclusivity means equal opportunity to combat discrimination, imbalances, injustices and under-representation.

If we can indeed let go of our outdated ideas to which we cling and often think we need and instead embrace the whole integral picture in this "evolutionary spirituality", then our way of being is changed even though many people still continue to work with and live within the old dualistic models.

There are visionaries, models, groups, and communities if we care to join and share the journey with others. These people must be those who are engaged in their own transformation; they are not on an ego-journey; they are authentic in their spirituality Praxis, walking the talk, so others can safely join and relate. Partnership and mutual relationship are hallmarks of these groups. We can learn from our earlier centuries, from those who have gone before us on the journey; our brothers and sisters–who in quantum terms of time and space, are still with us today.

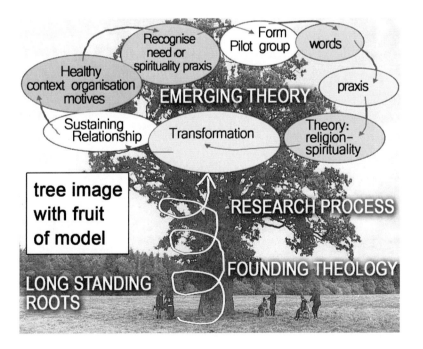

There is an understanding of certain points so that the on-going process can continue and therefore result in living spirituality praxis as individuals and groups.

1. It requires intentional social activity.
2. There is the need for emancipatory transformation.
3. We must live with relational power and collaboration,
4. Listening to marginalised people and those engaged in justice, peace and the integrity of creation who are bringing their agenda to the academy.
5. We must recognise and be aware of various personal wake up calls–for example, through illness, death, shock, insight or other realisations that can trigger a change of values and consciousness and
6. Recognise the need for interdependent Relationships, Transformation and Change.

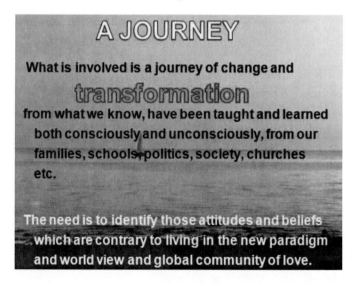

The diagram above is a visual representation of our journeys, depicting what happens if we choose to embrace change as we become more aware and conscious of what kind of life we are living both within and around us.

The essential understanding is to realise that we have all been "conditioned" in various ways from childhood onwards. We need to become aware and conscious of that conditioning which requires us to identify any attitudes or beliefs, which are unhelpful, unhealthy and even directly in opposition to the type of life of love that we are now choosing to live. It is very hard work and requires great commitment and support.

Subsequent questions and points for reflection which emerge are:

1. Can we dare to let ourselves be challenged by unjust, unequal situations, refugees, oppression, the poor, the earth and the environment?

2. The real journey takes place in the depths of our souls, in the depth of the human and cosmic journey in all its realms: psychological, social, cultural, political, economic, ecological and cosmological.

3. Such a journey is only possible in relation to the divine mystery, is never self-initiated, sustained or fulfilled since God empowers at each step as we surrender in love.

4. We need a large proportion of the human race to seek the path of wisdom if the world is to be preserved and so spiritual vision is not an elitist luxury but vital to our survival.

5. The danger is to sabotage our journey by becoming "spiritual tourists" – not committing ourselves to one path on a spiritual journey, because it *requires* patience, endurance, wisdom, courage and humility. "Spiritual tourists" risk slipping back into old habits and so waste years or a lifetime. (Dryer, 1993: 612-622) (Rinpoche, 1996) (Ruether, 1993) and (Byrne 1993:565-577)

We need to be able to take the blame for our deep-rooted attitudes that need radical change, facing the truth so that we can then relate to others sensitively and honestly and be able to love across social and religious barriers. This radical change requires transformation. (Lees, 1987)

Chapter 9

Nourishment for the Future

In the field of spirituality, few if any things provide a quick fix. With this realization comes a need for guidance. Below are guidelines for offering an understanding. These include points about what is involved in transformation and how to embrace and effect change in our lives as well as the lives of others.

Some of these identify the cost for being involved–the cost for living spiritually. Connecting our inner and outer spirituality ethic is difficult. Yet we need to struggle so that we can live an authentic spiritual life with renewed hearts. These new hearts seek, not power over others, but power with others.

Continuing research and study

Loving conduct is concrete, both meeting needs and addressing causes so that they may be eliminated. Therefore it is essential to study systems and issues to avoid shallowness or counter productiveness.

It is no longer appropriate for theologians to analyse objectively from within universities, but rather they could recognise that the pastoral ambience provides raw material. We must not be caught in enthusiasm about spirituality without making connections in our own experience.

Since spirituality can become secularised and psychologised credentials may be needed.

Good teachers for the journey

If we can speak from our own intrinsic authority we then are able to create the kind of theological living-space needed for search for meaning. As we speak from our own pain and passion for truth we can make the journey "with" others, while knowing that we facilitate the growth which the Spirit produces.

"Personal is political" challenges us to transform human relationships and institutions. Then the fruit of growth is that we can live in mutual participation with all persons, the earth, cosmos and God.

We will know by our resultant behaviour if we are living an "integrated spirituality" – if we are able to create new politics, able to generate new social structures and thus help to restore the whole fabric of life which has congruence between our inner and outer life and ethic. Our love will be connected to justice as we live with a paradigm of power which is one of mutual empowerment "with" others.

Use of words and language

Trying to discuss "spirituality" and come to some sort of common understanding was difficult for us and can be difficult because of the language, the words and the terminology used. Different theological or spiritual backgrounds can have different meanings of words used and often this is not discovered until much later. Since words and language can be an issue, we need to use simple language. Some people can't find the right "words" to share "felt" experiences.

It is unwise therefore to link the lives of many with stereotypical accounts of spirituality, since some people have language available to them and some don't and can therefore feel out of their depth.

If we can hear and respect people's experiences without judgement, they may eventually relate in terms of spiritual depth. It is important to listen for the depth of meaning in a language which is mostly metaphorical and not to "define" spirituality in terms of one kind of experience since it is an act of interpretation.

The name of God used to describe un-nameable Reality, often conjures up images of a super-human person. Church language implies a "God up there". Some believe that the crisis of faith today is not doctrinal but one of language. We need a language which can express the knowledge quantum physics and cosmology is giving us.

Our dominant culture restricts our language and capacity for speech. Theological language has been stripped of integrative qualities – is empty of emotion and is ghost-like. We need non-patriarchal and non-authoritarian language to describe God who is not distant, powerful and dominant. We need a language to take our emotions seriously so we can communicate experiences of God. "It is impossible to speak of what lies beyond the capabilities of speech–yet we feel compelled to speak of it". (Soelle 1994)

Thus language can feel like a prison because it can exclude others since some people have no language at all to describe their most important experiences. We must begin with experience instead and rediscover a new language with the "story" of human beings and experience, all the while being careful not to substitute another dominant exclusive language instead. Actually "words" used can often be projections of our own fear or insecurity. We may have to turn "language" on its head before we can grasp what the problem is.

The creative use of language then allows us to immerse ourselves in "God" or talk about "God" as the fundamental Love and depth. Symbols of nature often indicate a "relationship" of unity and belonging.

Organisational systems

Organisational systems often compete for exclusive divine approval and thus can cause feuds. In our workplaces people have opportunities in public and political situations to challenge and change systems which cause poverty. To do so requires a personal spiritual rhythm in our lives, since the goal of formation is one of compassion and loving kindness. Being called to advocacy and solidarity with those on the margins will often lead to conflict and collision with powerful institutions – both "Church" and "State" when they organise themselves against the weak.

Spiritual rhythm, discipline and spiritual practice

Purposive actions void of self-centredness are central to a spiritual rhythm in our lives. Founders of all major religions demonstrate a concern for helping others with love as the hallmark of their lives, teaching us to "practice" in love, compassion, respect and truth – free of ego.

Transformation of our own hearts and minds allows us to put our own spiritual teachings into practice.

With this understanding we are not following complicated dogmas but instead the doctrine of compassion, love and respect as we re-order our habits and attitudes. Love cannot be programmed; it does not come from human effort alone, but is the very core and centre of all authentic religion.

Accountability

Our ultimate goal is to help to change the hearts and minds of oppressors instead of just removing burdens from the oppressed. Our accountability is to the world which is battered and bruised by forces of patriarchy. We "are" accountable when we are attuned to the movements of the Spirit at work in the world with a priority of a relational and co-operative mode. Everything is interconnected and interrelated and so we can discard the dualistic construction of "sacred versus secular". We can transcend narrow and ideological confines of religions of power and fear.

Accountability includes the weak also being able to move from impotence to power "with" others, being able to move then from unconscious, unsuspecting tolerated impotence and able to confront life-threatening power.

Common global vision

The common global vision is one of a transformation of society, culture and consciousness. Since globalisation is based on the premise that the poor become poorer as the rich become abusively richer, there is therefore a need to live out and distribute justice and allocate resources appropriately.

Implications within our environment of increased spiritual awareness embracing values of empowerment, participation, inclusiveness, and sustainable development means social, political and financial consequences.

Guidelines for practising a transformational spirituality

A rightly understood and practiced spirituality might give direction and meaning to transformations of society, culture and consciousness. A "phenomenon of spirituality" could provide deepest energy resources for a new holistic spirituality, "a mysticism of action".

The aspects of the personal, social and global in an understanding of transformational spirituality are closely interdependent. Therefore the new paradigm would be a "transformative spirit in action" which integrates action and contemplation, social and personal, outward and inward.

Spirituality must permeate the personal and political, and animate our thought, action and imagination. There is an urgent need to work for a broader development of spiritual awareness among all peoples in order to be able to respond to the hope and the agonies of our suffering world.

Diversity, discrimination and equal opportunity

True spirituality should combat discrimination, imbalance, injustice, under-representation or exclusion by addressing the underlying issues and reasons for these injustices so that discriminatory barriers are removed. It can't be just tokenism or a faddish change of the way the institution looks on the surface.

It has to result rather in actual depth so there is equality.

We have to live out what we say thus avoiding discrepancies; we must allow people to be who they are while encouraging growth and fulfilment of their potential thus radically altering institutions which previously excluded people who felt marginalised.

A new vision for life

According to Soelle mysticism and community exist in complex tension with one another.

"Genuine mysticism" is revolutionary – going out into ongoing creation of the world in which we "participate", not isolating the personal and individual.

Two trends leading to spiritual difficulty are: globalisation and individualism. *Globalised* economic order coerces people to produce more at speed to profit 20 per cent of us with less interest in social and ecological webs in which we live. *Individualism* has no attachment to fellow creatures. The rich get richer at the expense of the poor.

There is a gap – consider ethics, basic human rights and environment. Some companies say one thing and do the opposite. There is a conflict between profitability and the environment and human rights.

However, there is also *a new vision for our life together* with groups who are committed to critical openness, voluntary effort and who can be bearers of hope as carriers of resistance since they employ a different interest than consumerism. They live with a "good practice" of corporate accountability and social and environmental responsibility.

Spirituality applied and practical orthopraxis in the face of globalisation and repression

Liberating movements express changes in practice and principles of liberation. Orthopraxis recognizes that the poor are our teachers by uncovering causes, standing up for justice and human rights and thus setting us free from economic, political, cultural and spiritual oppression.

Symptoms of our current disease, which is the result of and fruit of the long-standing mechanistic view of the universe, has taught us to control – and now there is a threat of planetary destruction.

The *Ancient world view* was of an integrated whole of physical, psychological and spiritual worlds interrelated and integrated to form a unity. We transcend dualities through transformation and a new state of consciousness along with a higher knowledge of the direct experience of the indwelling Spirit of God.

Modern physics tells us that the whole universe has to undergo a radical transformation. As consciousness develops we integrate rational mind and ego-consciousness and are able to become more of our true selves and relate more deeply. We emerge through all levels of consciousness – physical, emotional/imaginative, rational and transrational. We are able to live in a complicated web of interdependent relationships.

A *psychological revolution* is required to develop a humanely empowering vision. Inauthentic distortions in relationships have an unequal distribution of power which is not simply overcome with a reversal of power, because this would only cause further polarisation.

A *theology* "mysticism of liberation" holds on to the dignity and human rights of the destitute, makes no distinction between church or secular movements, recognises everything that exists co-exists and is bound up into a network of relationships called interdependence and coexistence. Love overcomes illusions of autonomy, self-sufficiency and a praxis of exclusion. This is already the hope of self-aware minorities.

The bigger mystical task is to remain living in the world while resisting the urge to possess power. Instead we can live with a true democratic mysticism of everyday life and help to take responsibility for everything which insults a sense of equality and justice, and address and oppose the causes of war in ourselves. We can then work to address underlying causes of oppression and be mutually inclusive of all people, recognising that we are not autonomous or self-sufficient but rather inter-dependent.

Genuine change

Evolutionary spirituality happens when we are thrown into a process of genuine change and transformation through feeling powerless, in an impasse. Therefore we have to move from an old to a new paradigm at personal, group, societal, national and international levels. We then need to search out a new understanding of God related to the intellectual, practical and ethical concerns of the present situation of all oppressed groups towards emancipative possibilities for the future.

This change is beyond conscious control and is not given on demand but only as we surrender in love. It is not a theory but an experience; it is not validating things as they are or a ploy to keep people contented as "outcasts" in a patriarchal land. We need rather to express our anger and rage, which purifies "abused consciousness" of all repressed possibilities and "lost alternatives", in compassion with all those who cry for liberation.

Maturing to wholeness as a complete person happens with the affirmation of self which comes from deep inside. Such a new "integrating spirituality" is capable of creating new bodies and generating new social structures.

Living spirituality in practice

Often our actual spiritual life and living lags behind our holy thoughts, aspirations and ability to "discuss" religious and moral questions.

What is love – how do we attain a quality of love? There is nothing we can do and if we do, it is forced, cultivated and phoney, for love cannot be forced.

Freedom could be another word for love which happens when we stop discriminating and dies at the moment of coercion, control or conflict. Love means being sensitive to life, things, persons and excluding nothing. Love removes blocks so that what is there can surface; it doesn't respond to prefabricated guidelines and principles but to concrete reality.

If we have an awareness of self and other we will know what love is. It means dropping what we have drawn from past conditioning and experiences and the control society has over us with tentacles penetrating to the roots of our being. They are categories, prejudices, projections, needs, attachments, labels and concepts.

What will save the world is not goodwill but a *change in our thinking.* Otherwise we respond to principles and ideologies, economic, political, religious and psychological belief systems, preconceived ideas, and prejudices with thinking contaminated with fear, desire, self-interest, consciously or unconsciously.

We *don't* need doctrinal formulations, methods, techniques, spiritual exercises or formulas. We *do need* hearts divested of programming because *spirituality* isn't lived by a practice of techniques but by being a certain kind of person. It is not a commodity you can buy. What matters is what you are and what you become.

On-going discernment process

Discernment is reflecting on experience and action taken within the context of a growing conversation about God's loving action in the world, which includes concern for the planet as we try to live a life of faith in a manner which promotes God's action in the world.

"Spirituality" is defined in terms of experience, reflection, decision and action and lays the basis for a "spirituality of action".

The Pastoral Cycle: On-going spiritual development and fruits

On-going spiritual development requires us to be whole hearted, prepared to go all the way with a determination to be transformed with no turning back. It is narrow and demanding, requires a condition of complete simplicity, demands not less than everything and is a process and breakthrough into love.

Spiritual development and its fruits are not separate little units but deeply interconnected, so that all we do, feel and endure has a secret effect, radiating far beyond ourselves. It introduces us into a vast "spiritual society" and offers us a choice.

Other thoughts

I like what Evelyn Underhill wrote in 1929. She said that:

1. It is not what we say or do, but what we are, which provides the medium through which God reaches others.
2. We each have a personal choice.
3. We can be live wires as links between God's grace and the world that needs it, but first we have to offer ourselves without conditions, as transmitters of God's enabling love.
4. Love is the budding point from which the rest and fruit come.

Our aim is:

1. to be in tune with our whole selves
2. to take up true responsibility where "we" choose
3. not to be thinking for others so we squeeze them into decisions
4. to be able to move beyond doctrinally narrow channels
5. to have a love and acceptance of people
6. to not just agree with the human point of view
7. to be able to deal with our cultural biases and

8. to take responsibility to change deep rooted attitudes which oppress others.

We do this by firstly accepting ourselves so that we can love others with respect – not imposing our culture on others.

The cost is *learning* how to be open and honest and being able to create an environment that brings life-giving relationships where people *"experience"* it with all their being. This depends on the quality of relationships, where feelings and thoughts are integrated so others experience the "tangible" nature of love and don't fall in the gap between what you "say" and what you "live out". This happens not only through "theory", but is evidenced in real experience and when we "are" what we are talking about, thus leading by life and example. We are then able to stand up for justice and peace.

Important principles to consider are to:

1. stand up against unjust institutions
2. struggle for peace and justice
3. take blame for deep rooted attitudes which need radical change
4. face the truth so we can relate to others sensitively and honestly
5. be able to love across social and religious barriers because holiness and social action are pre-requisites of each other
6. move beyond parochial and national concerns of globalisation and all challenges of war, chaos and self-destruction with a belief in human dignity and basic human rights
7. know the value of justice, freedom, peace and mutual respect, in love and generosity
8. use reason rather than force
9. realise that we need new structures and rearrangement of institutional relations

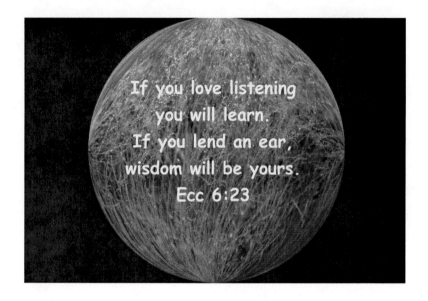

If you love listening
you will learn.
If you lend an ear,
wisdom will be yours.
Ecc 6:23

Chapter 10

Transformation and Love

We are all one

Learning together and interconnected

In a way of life, that is a life long journey of transformation

Not a religion, theology, ideology, theory, or dogma

It is who we are! Being.

Not just what we think and say, but what we live out in love

With consciousness and awareness.

A Quantum Parable

"Come into my den," said Mr. Fox to Mrs. Rabbit.

"Whatever for?" asked Mrs. Rabbit.

"Because I can give you three meals a day, a warm bed, someone to look after you, and security for life."

"Hmm!" said Mrs. Rabbit. "And after you fatten me up, you can eat me!"

"Come down my rabbit hole," said Mrs. Rabbit to Mr. Fox.

"Whatever for?" asked Mr. Fox.

"Because I can give you adventure, excitement, fulfilment, and uncertainty for life."

"Hmm!" said Mr. Fox.

"I think I'll stay with my den!"

(Geraldine O'Meara 2011)

Interview with Beatrice Bruteau

I read some of Beatrice Bruteau's writing, especially *A Song that Goes on Singing,* while I was doing my MA. I was very struck with the integration of her thinking and of her own life experience, practice and appropriation. She has a unique and multifaceted background that she brings to our contemporary understanding and life. I personally believe that what she is saying in the interview below is valid and worth listening to. In fact, this is the type of thinking I also began to embrace after all my own reading and study during the MA and I continue to believe it. Choice is such an important and vital element in the way forward for all of us. Also, this change and paradigm shift must be done globally as a society with enough people to make the shift work, which is what she is saying. So many people are now saying that.

I believe that what is written below, taken from her interview, is of vital importance and in a way serves as a summary to what I have learned and experienced over the past 14 years of formal study and 70 years of living.

Dr Bruteau has for the past 50 years or so been charting a unique path through the worlds of science, philosophy, mathematics, evolutionary theory and mysticism East and West. She is a practicing Catholic and has a unique understanding of the combination of the spiritual and scientific while seeking the mystical in the material and the vast creativity of God in the temporal unfolding cosmos.

She believes that we are at a unique juncture in history, suggesting that perhaps evolution will this time be one of a transformation of consciousness. She states that as human beings we are in a crucial position and that to take this next evolutionary step, we must become conscious participants in the unfolding of the evolutionary process. It all depends on what we choose to do as to whether the universe goes forward or falls back into entropy.

She believes that we are all filled with a mystical longing, for ultimate meaningfulness and in order to attain this in today`s climate we need a new theology of the cosmos – one that is grounded in the best science of our day, a theology where God is very present precisely *in* all the dynamism and patterns of the created order. We would see God as deeply involved in the evolutionary process of the world. Consciousness is the most God-like capacity, and consciousness is aware of the fact that it is consciousness.

Evolution carries with it an increase of consciousness and when the cosmic organization goes on to another level of complexity by uniting elements of the preceding level, which palaeontologist Teilhard de Chardin called "creative unions", they bring into being something that never *existed before*. The New Being emerges from the connections and interactions of the composing units and it constitutes a new level of oneness and wholeness.

It is because we can look back and see the pattern recurring that we can legitimately extrapolate and project the pattern into the future, according to Teilhard. Each time, there is an exchange of "Characteristic energy" among the uniting elements. Atoms are capable of making *connection* with one another and interact to form the union, so in order for us as human beings to unite with one another to form the next creative union ... we must share with one another our characteristic energies. It is the energy sharing that forms the bond. We now have *human energy* that is the energy of thinking, knowing, loving, willing and this most intimate energy is what we are asked to commit to the new union. The question is whether human beings will actually do this enough to form the next level of cosmic evolution.

We will not automatically unite since each of us is free; we can choose. So the next creative advance in evolution will only come about if we freely consent to form it because the energy exchange consists of free acts. It all hangs on our decision; *we are evolution.*

We bear a great responsibility. The capacity for a new kind of wholeness in the world is not from some outside force but it is inherent in the uniting elements, with their own power of communication, the power to unite with others to do things that we singly cannot do – she refers to forming a new kind of further Being.

We will have to redirect our energy currents. It will take energy even to make that option since our energy currents are "egocentric" flowing from the ego, grasping what is good for the ego, and flowing back to the ego. It tries to assimilate to all other human beings the being of the ego. If we don't make a big effort to realize the True Self, we will run entirely on the motives to exploit and dominate. These motives are endangering the world.

We must transcend our ego's impulses which keep us separate from each other. Self-realization is essential to form the next creative union to form a truly *New* Being, to unite to the deepest most central energies of consciousness. This depth is currently buried and hidden in most of us. We do various spiritual practices in the hope of becoming fully aware of our deep reality which is that place in the centre of our being. In meditation, we try to centre ourselves in our sense of existing without identifying with these descriptors. To the extent that we become acquainted to this, we may spontaneously behave in a new way.

Our energy is affected when we define ourselves in terms of qualities, which we then have to protect and try to gain more valuable ones like beauty, personality, wealth, power and social status. However if we liberate ourselves from such identity then all our energy becomes available for the radiation of goodwill to others. Each of us will have realized our self as the Self that says only I AM ... not a this or that.

You can say, "Let it be." Agape which seeks the well-being of others is an energy of love which is inexhaustible and streams out from us in every way. "Creative love" *is* a will to being; it is the ultimate energy of God and the intention is to *share being*. The truth of our being is continuous with the Divine Source of all reality. It is our participation in the *"glory of God"* that "fills the whole world". The next step in human evolution is cosmic evolution, which is the hidden Godness in us coming forth.

Human community and the collective is an integrative operation and medium by which the oneness is made out of the diversity and protects the diversity. We unite in order to create. A new human community will be some kind of entity, being, sharing their characteristic human energy – which is agape, knowledge, concern, creativity, inventiveness and all other human energies we have – all that interchange of energies bind us together into a community. When the whole community experiences and practices this kind of love, the crisscrossing energies form a net, and the net is the New Being that can do what the individuals that it is composed of could not do.

Diversity is also absolutely essential to the unity of the composed being, increasing the being of the whole, the richness, the beauty.

Our personal energies do not merge or become *submerged* in some amorphous whole. Rather it feels like *an intensification* of individuality. Bruteau's view of spiritual awakening is the foundation for an evolutionary progression toward ever-higher expressions of integration. That is when you find the I AM in the

Oppressors: in the old paradigm of power & worldview with its arrogant eye and stare:

Patriarchal system
Hierarchical dualism
and power
Aggressive social systems
- unilateral power
Power "over"
- domination
- Imperialism

A Paradigm shift requires us to move and change from "I" to "we" – to a new paradigm of "relational power" and collaboration.

Through a transformative journey and Psychological revolution

Oppressed:
Weak, submissive victims oppressed & Marginalized, vulnerable as "the other" objects
Subordinate & powerless

A CIRCLE OF FRIENDSHIP a model of reality with a new worldview and order an evolutionary spirituality which views with the Loving Eye in a circle of mutual connectedness and web of relationships – Living an "evolutionary spirituality"

An inclusive companionship paradigm for being in the world.

Living in a circle of companions and web of mutual and inclusive relationships, in true communion, with openness, respect, reciprocity, compassion, interdependence, interconnectedness, interrelationship, listening, love and compassion & co-operation with a passion for right relationship, care, empathy and concern.
It is deep, mutual and egalitarian.

None are superior or inferior since are lives are interwoven.

We live with integration, both/and,. empowering "with" others equally and in solidarity with recognition of "the other" with radical unity and diversity and transformed loving, in democratic and interactive relationships.

Friendship in a non-hierarchical web of relations, linked in generative web of communion with each other and rest of creation, in a great web of interbeing, and web of connectedness,which implies shared risk and co-operative evolutionary learning.

Respect for process, synthesis, the holistic, felt, experiential, affective, intuitive, metaphorical and bottom up growth, living in a Co-creative dance of human body/ mind and cosmos.

centre of yourself, you discover its intention is toward becoming and that is the evolution part.

If you really wake up, the deep Self in you is the Absolute, the Infinite, the Eternal, the Divine and it's manifesting as the particular human being that you're embodied as at the present time.

An expanding universe is a song that goes on singing; we sing not in order to come to the end of it. There is no defined goal – life fulfils itself precisely by never coming to an end. Everyone is absolutely essential and infinitely precious, since the process of forming the next Great Step in evolution, which is the manifestation of the Infinite One, requires that we ourselves voluntarily, consciously and intentionally do the interactions that will constitute the energy exchanges that *make* the New Being.

From now on if we are to have any future, we *must create that future for ourselves*. We ourselves are the future and we are the revolution.

Bruteau, B (2002)

Conclusion

How This Book Came About

Ever since completing my doctorate I have wanted to be able to share some of what we learned, especially with regard to the field of spirituality and its connection to the expanding field of science, that is Quantum Physics. I began to read about and make these connections during my M.A. and then in the doctorate. Since then I have continued to research and study in both these fields. This book is a response to that desire, written for the general public, rather than as an academic paper.

By way of a further, more academic introduction, I want to share a brief summary or the essence of my formal studies, both for the MA in Christian Spirituality and the Doctorate in Professional Studies, because that has been the overriding and long-standing impetus for this book. Additionally, because Spirituality is still a relatively new academic field I thought that outlining this learning would help others to understand more of what is involved.

At Heythrop (1997-1999), I studied three terms: (1) Foundations for the Study of Spirituality; (2) Patterns of Spiritual Formation and Human Development; and (3) Women's Spirituality. Not surprisingly, a small group of students came together to discuss and share each week what we were learning experientially, how we were being touched emotionally and how we were beginning to be able to "appropriate" what we were learning.

We all had different impressions, preferences in reading, and therefore different essay choices and discussions. We all came from different backgrounds and experiences and brought all that to the classes and incorporated them into our essay choices and content. It was fascinating. I had no idea what spirituality meant, really. We studied/read writers from the fifteenth and sixteenth centuries as well as more current writers. There was more importance placed on womens' spirituality because of the growing realization that women were and are oppressed worldwide and over the centuries. We studied Third World spirituality, how spirituality was different from theology, the part that language and words played in the whole discipline because it was so difficult to come up with adequate terminology to explain and converse within this new field.

Our minds were reeling, and we complained that we didn't understand the words we were reading and had to have a dictionary to hand all the time. The massive amount of reading was difficult to get through and in the midst of all this we were each changing as we absorbed the material, input, discussions and application at different levels. It touched us all deeply, emotionally and spiritually. We were confused and having to adjust the things that we were taught and told previously in our lives, that is, "this is the way it is and the way it ought to be," and try to determine if these were consistent with the truths that we were now realising and learning.

I was beginning to discover more deeply the truth indeed was that things were often not "as they ought to be" but rather were the opposite. We also learned that our Earth Home, the Cosmos and all living beings were part of our web of relationships. The charity I was working with which the community founded, was situated on 350 acres of virgin land, and this special environment was an important aspect of what we were offering there. We had a short-term residential place for disabled people and carers (caregivers), and so we constructed accessible paths, purchased various vehicles they could use and offered environmental instruction and experience. I did my dissertation on what impact the environment had during the personal interaction the guests had within that environment.

Our lecturer circulated a paper, written in 1988 by Danah

Zohar on Quantum Physics. I questioned if what Zohar wrote was really true, then why wasn't everyone, everywhere, jumping up and down? It seemed so relevant and totally exciting and important. She replied that it takes most people years.

All of what I was learning seemed shocking. I had no idea that spirituality was so different from theology; our tutor said we were so lucky to get in on this field at the beginning. I had no idea either what that meant or of the extreme importance of her statement. It took many years for me to really comprehend. Spirituality was talked about as a slippery eel, a minefield, and an academic subject in its own right but sadly still remained "under" the department of Theology within Universities the world over. It was so exciting, challenging, new, vast, academically demanding and transformative personally. It turned my life upside down, as it did to others of us in the class of twenty or so.

My appetite was totally whetted for more such learning and resultant life-style change and understanding with others. Most people I knew and those in the community referred more to "theology" and couldn't understand the difference of the meaning of the word spirituality, which for me was vast. I got isolated to some degree but remained totally excited and passionate about studying more in order to continue to learn and appropriate what I was learning.

I became more and more passionate about studying, that is to learn more deeply and to be able to appropriate what I was learning. I especially began to discover more deeply the truth that indeed things were often not "as they ought to be" but rather the opposite. We also learned the importance of our Earth Home, the Cosmos and that all living beings are part of our web of relationships. Power "over" people was not an authentic, healthy or loving way of living but neither was living in oppression and "under" the Dominance of Patriarchy.

By then I also had several major questions about my own context and how to truly appropriate and live out my own new deep learning. I began to see so many places where an authentic way of life was being lived out, which presented so many challenges to me. The suggestion was to see things through the lens of our contexts. Since we had studied Third World spirituality, women's spirituality, the church structure and context and the concern for the environment, I could no longer, for the sake of justice and integrity, ignore what I saw and experienced. I began to challenge and ask questions of any seemingly unhealthy, inauthentic contexts which stated one thing and practiced another, because those structures were oppressive.

The diagram below highlights just a few of the key words that became very relevant and meaningful.

Spirituality is understood at personal and social levels. It is both a personal experience and taught at university levels. It is different from theology, religion, and church but is not defined

Personal & social   understood from where you are

A new academic subject   slippery eel

The breath of life   the Spirit   mine-field

Newtonian since 1600's

Living in a web-of-relationships

Experiential

Sustaining our Earth Home & Cosmos   Live out what you say

by any one of them. Spirituality includes all of life, is all of life and therefore includes our shared earth home. None of us are separate from it; we are all part of the web of life; we are all connected. Some are more in touch with the depths of and reality of the Spirit and others prefer to stay within their thoughts and head because of fear. No one faith or denomination or religion owns spirituality.

The fruit and insights of such study changed my life at a deep level. It was transformative only in as much as I chose to take on board and live out that which I was learning. I still find the material and what I learned and still learn from it so exciting and revealing. The writers are tremendous and very experienced teachers so I learned a great deal from them. In each term I wrote two essays and at the end a Dissertation, the content of which is included as appropriate, within the previous pages of this book.

My passion to continue to learn grew within me so I decided to do a PhD (2000-2003) and had several choices, but soon realised that this type of individual study would isolate me even more from my community, so I searched for and found a place where the study was work based as a relevant, live project. It also had to be officially requested in writing by the work place as a necessary project for research within the organization, along with three other references within the field or profession, indicating and verifying the need for such research within the field of spirituality by *The National Centre for Work Based Learning Partnerships at Middlesex University London.*

I was accepted and there were of course various stakeholders then: the trustees of the Charity, the Director, my Community, and the three other prominent "professionals" in the field of spirituality, as well as the University with its own Doctoral level Descriptors and of course my Academic tutors, one for the "Project" and one for the discipline of Spirituality. Having so many stakeholders was very challenging indeed.

It was a massive, complex project, about which the intake interviewers at the university commented. Of course, I didn't really understand what they meant. All along as a research group within our organization, we also looked at where we were situated in our personal, groups and organizational lives and noted discrepancies in the various structures that we had to challenge. We had to walk the talk at personal, group, and organizational levels. The metaphor of a tree with bottom up growth happening from the founding roots up the trunk and eventually bearing fruit on the branches and leaves continued to be very useful and relevant. Spirituality was a challenge at every level. It wasn't thought and mind-oriented theology but rather living by the Spirit of Love, as the measuring rod and life-giving source and so we could have our lives informed through "living theory".

The doctorate asked the research question, "How can Holton Lee best establish a Spirituality Praxis?" Thus began our four-year research project. As previously stated, I first had to design a research methodology, because doing qualitative research with questionnaires would not suffice. I was studying a way of life. So I combined various approaches which were quite cyclical, Participative Action Research, the Learning Cycle, the Discernment Cycle, the Heuristic Approach and I functioned as an Ethnographer,while attempting to keep my hands off the "process", that is trying not to influence the process which was happening with the six of us in the research group.

Guests, trustees, volunteers, staff and the research group were all interviewed. One of the doctoral descriptors required deep third level learning and change within the research project, in our real living project, taking place in a real situation and part of the outcome was developing "living theory". It was a deep challenge for us and certainly one that led to deep change in all of us personally and in the research group and organisation. We all, it seemed, had to change, grow, be more open and willing to hear new ways, question old ways, learn from each other, be willing to listen and read masses of material and books in order to be an informed reading group who could research together. I was not the "leader" but a member of the group that I facilitated.

I began our research by designing a diagram of a tree, that is the image or metaphor that was emerging and then it gave us a basic understanding and also can continue to do so for some of the many people interested and working within the field of spirituality. I did this in order to give a starting point of experience and an overview for us as a research group and for subsequent readers who were coming to the subject cold, as it were. Then I moved on to explain the key word in the research question, which was "Praxis". We continued on then discovering together the differences between religion, theology and spirituality, which is often a very confusing point for people. The last part of chapter 1 is an overview of a broad understanding of what the word *spirituality* means to various writers and others. In fact, there was and still is such a broad spectrum from A to Z, from Fundamentalism to New Age, and everything in between. So, my doctoral journey of learning seemed to be a big risk, challenge, desire, and passion that seemed overwhelming most of the time.

Some theory emerged from our bottom up research process as we used the metaphor of a tree, with the long standing history of the land and project continuing to provide nourishment, wisdom, insight and along with current and relevant experience moving up from the roots through the trunk and out into the branches, eventually bearing healthy and authentic fruit. This theory was the result of hours of conversation, process, reading, supervision, experience at personal, group and organizational levels that resulted in deep learning, change and transformation at so many levels.

In this book, I am also sharing what I learned over the past fifteen years of study and experience as well as my personal lifelong searching, living, journeying in my own spiritual life. I have been very passionate about my studies and even more passionate now in my desire and attempt to share what I have "learned" at a deeper level. However, it is hard to articulate and give voice to it especially since our "spiritual journey" is personal as well as being social. So there is no particular definition of it. During our research within the Charity, after three years of processing, we had a facilitator for a day to help us write out a very brief "spirituality statement" only, not a definition. We had to go over it word by word and it took all day so all six of us could be of one mind. This was after hours and years of conversation, process, reading, supervision, on-going experience and appropriation at personal, group and organizational levels that resulted in deep learning, change and transformation. We learned different ways of knowing which may also be useful coat pegs for readers to hang their thoughts and experiences on.

I really want to emphasize that one of the first and key understandings for me in considering the research question and methodology design was to understand *praxis.* That is I learned that if you combine theory and practice you get praxis, which is theory-informing practice and practice informing theory. That is true in the field of spirituality as in any field. I realized that we could learn a new, relevant and authentic theory of spirituality, which then would inform our living, and in turn our living experience would shape and inform our theory about spirituality.

So this seemingly simple word *spirituality* took four years to research, with a group that had many stakeholders as previously described.

I haven't been the same since those seven years of formal study. In particular, I now see all things through the lens of the context in which I am situated. The two models that emerged and developed during the research process, which I have now shared in this book, can be used in any situation and were the heart of our research cycles. I also developed many and various other diagrams during the research to help elucidate what was happening in the long process we were in. Words so often failed! Trustees and other staff were questioning why it was all taking so long,

I learned then and have found in the past years since then that it has become even more complicated, as a field, as well as something personal to me and others. I have learned that people are still seeking in all sorts of places, that I have changed deeply inside, learning how to "be", to let go, to embrace what I have learned and try to live it out. I have learned that systems which are dominant, top-down, power hungry, unjust, not living out right relationships still proliferate, causing lots of suffering throughout the world. I have learned that no one owns spirituality – that it is not a theory or dogma but rather inclusive – not an institution or place, or new. The Spirit is the Creator, Giver and Sustainer of life and is illusive and real.

It is now 2013, and I have now lived in Canada since 2005. I still come across so many people who say that they don't know what spirituality is or means to them. They are searching for an understanding of their own spirituality, seemingly not having found it in the churches or within other religious practices, in a relevant and meaningful way. Many of them find themselves searching on the margins and edges in so many places. The whole field of spirituality seems to have become even more confusing over the years as more and more self-styled gurus and other teachers from various other disciplines begin to put forward their concepts and understanding of spirituality.

Vulnerable people flock to them; some are helped and some are further confused. There seems to be a lack of oversight, authenticity and cohesiveness about what is happening within the field. There are so many websites, organizations, cyber-communities, courses, on-line courses with call-in group teachings and discussions because today there are far less confines and restrictions of space and time. More people also are now aware about how much Quantum Mechanics affirms our spirituality, which is helpful and reassuring.

No one denomination, faith, or doctrine has ownership of spirituality since the Spirit is inclusive and not exclusive. Language continues to be a great divider in our global understanding of the Divine, Other, One, Unnameable, Spirit, One,

Higher Power, Mystery or Love. Often it is only a matter of language difference not doctrine.

On our spiritual or life journeys of body, mind, and spirit, people are exploring spirituality, consciousness and awareness-raising, often too for the sake of our Earth Home, recognising that we are in a global crisis at so many and escalating levels. The on-going and increasingly important stated need, is to gather together enough people , somehow, who have this shared intent, so we can all become more healthy, integrated and authentic as individuals and collectively and so that more sound and healthy decisions can be made within our personal and global lives and home.

Praxis became the main component and shaped our research journey and continues to be a very important influencing tool within my life today. And so I continue my journey.

Bibliography

This bibliography is extensive and can therefore be a useful resource for readers to choose books they find relevant to their areas of interest.

There is also an extensive website section. This comprises groups that are gathering together all around the world in order to develop communities of interest and thought as a resource to themselves and others. They often put on conferences, workshops and some of them make the content available to download. Some are now beginning to develop on-line courses and webinars and are publishing books.

There are also several suggested YouTube video teachings, which are helpful in a different way. They cover areas such as spirituality and spirituality and physics. There is so much available on the web today; it has become a virtual library and also a maze to sort through.

Abram, D (1997) *The Spell of the Sensuous.* New York: Vintage Books

Armsby, P (2000) *"Methodology in Work Based Learning."* In Work Based Learning and the University: New Perspectives and Practices. Portwood, D and Costely, C (eds) Birmingham: SEDA Paper 109

Au, W (1990) *By Way of the Heart, Toward a Holistic Christian Spirituality.* London: Geoffrey Chapman

Au, W (1995) *"The Teaching of Spirituality in the Formation Programme of Religious Orders."* In The Way Supplement 84 Endean, P (ed), London: The Way Publications

Au, W (1993) *"Holistic Spirituality."* In The New Dictionary of Catholic Spirituality. Downey, M (ed) Minnesota: The Liturgical Press

Baksa, P (2011) *The Point of Power: Change Your Thoughts, Change*

Your Life, Intelegance Publishing.

Barnes, C (1998) *The Social Model of Disability.* In The Disability Reader. Social Science Perspectives Shakespeare, T (ed) London: Cassell

Bell, J (1999) *Doing Your Research Project A guide for first-time researchers.* In Education and Social Science, Buckingham: Open University Press

Berry, T (1999) *The Great Work. Our Way into the Future.* New York: Bell Tower

Biberman, J, and Whitty, M (eds) (2000) *Work and Spirit. A Reader of New Spiritual Paradigms for Organisation.* Scranton: The University of Scranton Press

Biberman, J, Whitty, M, Robbins, L (2000) *Lessons from Oz.* In Work and Spirit, Biberman, J and Whitty, M (eds), Scranton: The University of Scranton Press

Boje, D (2000) *Festivalism at Work: Toward Ahimsa in Production and Consumption.* In Work and Spirit, Biberman, J and Whitty, M (eds) Scranton: The University of Scranton Press

Breateau, B (2002) (http://www.enlightennext.org/magazine /j21/j21.asp)

Brown, P (2002) *The Earth Summit gets underway with 400 issues still to be resolved.* In the Guardian 26 August, page 1, The Guardian

Burton-Christie, D (1994) *Mapping the Sacred Landscape: Spirituality and the Contemporary Literature of Nature.* In Horizons 21/1 22-47, Horizons

Byrne, R (1993) *Journey (Growth and Development in Spiritual Life).* In The New CAFOD Campaign (1989-91) *Renewing the Earth–Study Guide for Groups.* London: The Catholic Fund for Overseas Development

Cashmore, G and Puls, J (1995) *Soundings in Spirituality.* Milton Keynes: The Living Spirituality Network

Cavanaugh, G (2000) *Spirituality for Managers.* In Work and Spirit Biberman, J and Whitty, M (eds) Scranton: The University of

Scranton Press

Chittester, J (1990) *Job's Daughters – Women and Power.* New Jersey: Paulist Press

Chopp, R (1993) *Praxis.* In the New Dictionary of Catholic Spirituality, Downey M, (ed) Minnesota: The Liturgical Press

Clarke, C (1996) *Reality through the Looking-Glass. Science and Awareness in the Postmodern World,* Edinburgh: Floris Books

Clarke, I (Ed) (2001) *Psychosis and Spirituality. Exploring the new frontier,* London: Whurr

Clarkson, P (1993) *Gestalt Counselling in Action.* London: Sage Publications

Clarkson, P *What is Learning by Enquiry. Http://www. physis.co.uk/pc/what_islearning_by_enquiry.htm#_ftn1* (Accessed 2.5.2000)

Clarkson, P (1998) *Developing Epistemological Consciousness About Complexity–Seven Domains of Discourse. Http://www.physis .co.uk/complexity_domains.htm (Accessed 2.5.2002)*

Clouser, R (1999) *Knowing with the Heart: Religious Experience and Belief in God.* Illinois: Intervarsity Press

Coghlan, D and Brannick, T (2001) *Doing Action Research in Your Own Organisation.* London: Sage Publications

Coghlan, D (2002) *Seminar on Action Research In Applied Spirituality Research.* At Milltown Institute, 5th July 2002, Working paper

Coghlan, D (1999) *Good Instruments: Ignatian Spirituality, Organisation Development and the Renewal of Ministries.* Rome: Society of Jesus

Coghlan, D (2001b) *Ignatian Teamwork: An Emergent Framework from the Instructions for the Team at Trent.* In Review of Ignatian Spirituality, 98, XXX11/111 2001, 65-74, Review of Ignatian Spirituality

Costley, C (2000) *The Boundaries and Frontiers of Work Based Knowledge.* In Work Based Learning and The University: New Perspectives and Practices, Portwood, D and Costley, C (eds)

Birmingham: SEDA Paper 109

Covey S and Merrill, A (1994) *First Things First.* London: Simon and Schuster Ltd

Critten, P (1998) *Management or Professional Development: A Rethink of Development in the Workplace Based on Complexity and Diversity Rather than Driven by the Control Agenda.* Paper given at a Conference on Emergent Field in Management: Connecting and Learning Critique, University of Leeds, July 15-17

Critten, P (2002) *Caring and Sharing—the Heart of a Community of Practice.* Paper given at a Conference Middlesex University Business School, February, 2002

De Mello, A (1993) *Call to Love–Meditations.* India, Gujarat Sahitya Prakash, Anad

Dick, B *Thesis Resource Paper You want to do an Action Research Thesis? Http://www.scu.edu.au/schools/gcm/ar/art/arthesis.html* (accessed 22.12.2000)

Dollard, K (2002) *Return of the Corporate Soul.* In The Tablet, Wilkins, J (ed) London: The Tablet, 27 July

Doncaster, K (1999) *Resource Pack for Reflecting On Learning within Work Based Learning Studies Programmes.* London: National Centre for Work Based Learning Partnerships

Downey, M (ed.) (1993) *The New Dictionary of Catholic Spirituality.* Minnesota: The Liturgical Press

Downey, M (1997) *Understanding Christian Spirituality.* New York: Paulist Press

Downey, M and Vanier, J (1986) *Recovering the Heart.* In Spirituality Today Winter 1986, Vol 38 *Http://www/spirituality-today.org/spirit2day/863844downey.html* (accessed 26.4.2001)

Dryer, E (1993) *Love.* In The New Dictionary of Catholic Spirituality, Downey, M (ed) Minnesota: The Liturgical Press

Dryer, E (2000) *Tensions in Spirituality.* In Spirituality Vol 6 November/December, Jordan, T (ed) Dublin: Dominican Publications and Orbis

Dubay, T (2002) *Realising my Inner Poverty* In Living Faith, Vol 18, Number Two, Neilsen, M (ed) Missouri: Creative Communications for the Parish

Edwards, F (1995) *"Spirituality, Consciousness and Gender Identification: A Neo-Feminist Perspective."* In Religion and Gender, King, U (ed) Oxford: Blackwell

Eisler, R and Loye, D (1990) *The Partnership Way.* San Francisco: Harper

Ely, M, Vinz, R, Downing, M and Anzul, M (2001) *On Writing Qualitative Research: Living by Words.* London: RoutledgeFalmer

Fisher, K (1995) *Women at the Well.* London: SPCK

Fitzgerald, C (1996) *"Impasse and Dark Night."* In *Women's Spirituality,* Wolski-Conn, J (ed) New York: Paulist Press

Freeman, L (2002) *A Letter from Lawrence Freeman OSB.* In the Christian Meditation Newsletter, Summer 2002 Ryan, G (ed) London: International Centre of The World Community for Christian Meditation

Freeman, L (2001) *How do the Gospel Stories affect us and Change our lives?* In The Christian Meditation Newsletter, July. Ryan, G (ed) London: International Centre of the World Community for Christian Meditation

Gablik, S (1998) *The Reenchantment of Art.* New York: Thames and Hudson

Gallagher, B (1988) *Meditations with Teilhard De Chardin.* Santa Fe, New Mexico: Bear & Company

Gibbons, P (2000) *Spirituality at Work: Definition.* In Work and Spirit Biberman, J and Whitty, M (eds) Scranton: The University of Scranton Press

Gillespie, K (2000) *Keeping Close Watch.* In MS Matters, Nov/Dec 2000 Issue No 34 MS Matters Magazine

Goswami, Ph.D., Amit (2011) *How Quantum Activism Can Save Civilization.* Charlottesville, VA: Hampton Roads Publishing Company, Inc.

Greenspan, M (1993) *A New Approach to Women and Therapy*. PA: TAB Books

Grey, M.C. (2003) *Sacred Longings: Ecofeminist Theology and Globalization*. London: SCM Press

Griffiths, B (1989) *A New Vision of Reality. Western Science, Eastern Mysticism and Christian Faith*. London: Collins

Handy, C (1988) *Understanding Voluntary Organisations*. London: Penguin Books

Hay, D (2001) *The Spiritual Life of People Who Don't go to Church*. In Living Spirituality Network News July, 2001 Milton Keynes: The Living Spirituality Network

Heaton, T (2001) *Disability Art, Why?* For the occasion of the 'generate' Exhibition at the Ferns Art Gallery 5 May–1 July 2001 Hull: Hull Museums and Art Gallery

Heron, J (1998) *Sacred Science. Person-centred Inquiry into the Spiritual and the Subtle*. Ross-on-Wye: PCCS Books

Heron, J (1996) *Co-Operative Inquiry Research into the Human Condition*. London: Sage Publications

Higgins, M and Letson, D (2002) *Power and Peril. The Catholic Church at the Crossroads*. Toronto: HarperCollins Publishers Ltd

Hinton, J and Price, P (2003) *Changing Communities. Church from the Grassroots*. London: Churches Together in *Britain and Ireland*

Hogan, L (2000) *A Framework for the Practical Application of Spirituality at Work*. In Work and Spirit Biberman, J and Whitty, M (eds) Scranton: The University of Scranton Press

Holloway, R (1997) *Dancing on the Edge: Faith in a Post-Christian Age*. London: Fount

Holmes, C (2002) *Book Review of the Spirited Business*. In GreenSpirit, Winter 2002 Hardy, J and Mowll, I (eds) London: The Association for Creation Spirituality

Hughes, G W (1993) *Oh God, Why? A Journey Through Lent for Bruised Pilgrims*. Oxford: The Bible Reading Fellowship

Hughes, G W (2002) "The Fourfold Grid on Finding Our Way in Spirituality." In Living Spirituality Network News January 2002 Milton Keynes, The Living Spirituality Network

Jenkins, L *A Chance to Touch the Trees.* In Yes Magazine, pp 18-19 Yes Magazine

Johnson, E (1998) *Friends of God and Prophets: A Feminist Theological Reading of the Communion of Saints.* London: SCM Press

Johnson, E (1993) *Women, Earth and Creator Spirit.* Madeleva Lecture New York: Paulist Press

Johnston, W (2000) *Arise, My Love. Mysticism for a New Era.* New York: Orbis Books

Keating, T and others (2008) *Spirituality, Contemplation & Transformation, Writings on Centering Prayer.* New York: Lantern Books

King, U (1992) *"Spirituality, Society and Culture."* In The Way Supplement 73 Lonsdale, D and Sheldrake, P (eds) London: The Way Publications

King, U (1995) *Religion and Gender.* Oxford: Blackwell

King, U (2008) *The Search for Spirituality: Our Global Quest for a Spiritual Life.* New York: Blueridge

King, S, Biberman, J Robbins, L and Nichol, D (2000) *Integrating Spirituality into Management Education in Academia and Organisations: Origins, a Conceptual Framework and Current Practices.* In Work and Spirit Biberman, J and Whitty, M (eds) Scranton: The University of Scranton Press

Kornfield J, (2000) *After the Ecstasy the Laundry. How the Heart Grows Wise on the Spiritual Path.* London: Rider

Krieger, M and Hanson, B (2000) *A Value-Based Paradigm for Creating Truly Healthy Organisations.* In Work and Spirit Biberman, J and Whitty, M (eds) Scranton: The University of Scranton Press

Lane, B (1992) *Landscape and Spirituality: A Between Place and Tension Placelessness in Christian Thought.* In The Way

Supplement No 73, Spring (Londsale, D and Sheldrake P, (ed) London: The Way Publications

Lane, B (1998) *The Solace of Fierce Landscapes.* New York: Oxford University Press

Lazarus, M (1998) *Preface.* In The Spirit of Science: from Experiment to Experience Edinburgh: Floris Books

Laszlo, Ervin (2008) *Quantum Shift in the Global Brain, How the New Scientific Reality Can Change Us and Our World.* Rochester, Vermont: Inner Traditions

Lees, F (1987) *Becoming the Kingdom: A vision of hope for the future.* Baskingstoke: Marshall Pickering

Lees, F and Hinton, J (1978) *Love is Our Home. The Beginnings of the Post Green Community.* London: Hodder and Stoughton

Lees, F and Nobbs, V (1982) *Break Open my World: Personal renewal for today.* London: Marshalls

Lees, T and Hinton, J (1980) *Another Man.* London: Hodder and Stoughton

Lonsdale, D (1996) *Listening to the Music of the Spirit: The Art of Discernment.* Notre Dame: Ave Maria Press

Lorimer, D (ed) (1998) *The Spirit of Science.* Edinburgh: Floris Books

Manazan, M et al (1996) *Women Resisting Violence Spirituality for Life from Experiment to Experience.* New York: Orbis Press

Masson, R (1984) *Spirituality for the Head, Heart, Hands, and Feet: Rahner's Legacy.* In Spirituality Today, Winter 1984 Vol 36, No 4, pp 340-354 *Http://www/spirituality today.org/spir2day/843645masson.html* (accessed 26. 2001)

Matthew, I (1995) *The Impact of God: Soundings from St John of the Cross.* London: Hodder and Stoughton

Matthews, M (2000) *Both Alike to Thee: The Retrieval of the Mystical Way.* London: SPCK

McAinsh, B (2003) *Introduction.* In Living Spirituality News Milton Keynes: The Living Spirituality Network, Spring 2003

McFague, S (2001) *Life Abundant. Rethinking Theology and Economy for a Planet in Peril.* Minneapolis: Fortress Press

McFague, S (1997) *Super, Natural Christians: How We Should Love Nature.* Minneapolis: Fortress Press

McFague, S (1993) *The Body of God: An Ecological Theology.* London: SCM Press

McNiff, J, Lomax, P, and Whitehead, J (1996) *You and Your Action Research Project.* London: Routledge

Midgley, S (2002) *Why God is Moving in the Workplace.* In Open Eye Magazine May 2002 Open University: Open Eye Magazine

Moustakas, C (1990) *Heuristic Research–Design, Methodology, and Applications.* London: Sage Publications

Neal, J, Bergmann Lichtenstein, B, Banner, D (2000) *Spiritual Perspectives on Individual, Organisational and Societal Transformation.* In Work and Spirit Biberman, J and Whitty, M (eds) Scranton: The University of Scranton Press

Noffke, S (1993) *Study.* In The New Dictionary of Catholic Spirituality Downey, M (ed) Minnesota: The Liturgical Press

Nouwen, H (1994) *In the Name of Jesus Reflections on Christian Leadership.* London: Darton, Longman and Todd Ltd

O'Murchu, D (2000) *Religion in Exile: A Spiritual Vision for the Homeward Bound.* Dublin: Gateway

O'Donohue, J (1997) *Anam Cara.* London: Bantam Press

O'Murchu, D (2002) *"At Home in God's Universe: An Interview with Diarmuid O'Murchu."* In Presence – The Journal of Spiritual Directors International Vol 8: No 1 Mabry, J (ed) California: Spiritual Directors International

O'Murchu, D and Sacks, J (2003) *The Religious Requirements.* Radio Four programme and interview. Mark Tully – 9 March Something Understood – Radio 4

O'Murchu, D (2004) *Quantum Theology – Spiritual Implications of the New Physics.* New York: The Crossroad Publishing Company

Parffrey, V *"Leadership by the Spirit?"* Http://www.arasite.org/vpl

.html (accessed 4.4.2001)

Pinney, L (2001) *Country Life.* The Times, Saturday July 14 p14

Portwood, D and Thorne, L (2000) *"Methodology in Work Based Learning."* In Work Based Learning and the University: New Perspectives and Practices. Portwood, D and Costely, C (eds) Birmingham: SEDA Paper 109

Principe, W (1993) *Christian Spirituality.* In the New Dictionary of Catholic Spirituality, Downey, M (ed) Minnesota: The Liturgical Press

Ravindra, R (2000) *Science and Wisdom-Compassion.* In Network, The Scientific and Medical Network Review, No 74 December 2000, Lorimer, D (ed) Surrey: Scientific and Medical Network

Reason, P and Bradbury, H(eds) 2001 *Introduction.* Handbook of Action Research Participative Inquiry and Practice London: Sage Publications

Reason, P (1994) Three Approaches to Participative Inquiry. *http://www.bath.ac.uk/~mnspwr/PAPERS/YVONNA.htm* (accessed 01.12.01)

Reason, P (1991) *Power and Conflict in Multidisciplinary Collaboration. http://www/bath.ac.uk/~mnspwr/PAPERS/POWER .htm* (accessed 01.12.01)

Regan, F (2001) *Millennium Christians.* In Vocation for Justice Spring, 2001, Vol 15 No 1 Nally, F (ed) London: Missionary Society of St Columban (Maynouth Mission to China)

Reinharz, S (1992) *Feminist Methods in Social Research.* Oxford: Oxford University Press

Rinpoche, S (1996) *The Tibetan Book of Living and Dying.* London: Rider

Rolheiser, R (1994) *The Shattered Lantern: Rediscovering God's Presence in Everyday Life.* London: Hodder and Stoughton

Ruffing, J (1993) *"Power."* In The New Dictionary of Catholic Spirituality Downey, M (ed) Minnesota: The Liturgical Press

Ruether, R (1998) *"Feminist Theologies in the Twentieth Century."* In Women and Redemption: A Theological History Minneapolis:

Fortress Press

Ruether, R (1993) *Sexism and God-Talk: Toward a Feminist Theology.* Boston: Beacon Press

Ruumet, H (1997) *Pathways of the Soul: A Helical Model of Psychospiritual Development.* In Presence–the Journal of Spiritual Directors International Vol 3: No 3 Mabry, J (ed) California: Spiritual Directors International

Schneiders, S (2000) *With Oil in Their Lamps: Faith, Feminism, and the Future.* New York: Paulist Press

Schneiders, S (1999) *"Articles on Theology: Mapping the Terrain." http://www.ihmsisters.org/spirituality-theological.html* (accessed 3 August, 2001)

Schneiders, S (1994) *"A Hermeneutical Approach to The Study of Christian Spirituality."* In Christian Spirituality Bulletin Spring 1994, Vol 2, No 1 Journal of the Society for the Study of Christian Spirituality

Seabrook, J (2002) *Sustainable Development is a Hoax: We Cannot Have it All, Unlimited Desire is Bound to Destroy a World of Limited Resources.* In the Guardian, 5 August, 2002, Page 16 London: The Guardian

Sheldrake, P (1998) *Spirituality and Theology: Christian Living and the Doctrine of God.* London: DLT

Sheldrake, P (1993) *Interpretation.* In The New Dictionary of Catholic Spirituality Downey, M (ed) Minnesota: Liturgical Press

Smith, A (2002) *"Narrow Vision: Cause of and Crisis of Faith."* In Spirituality Vol 8 No 41 Jordan, T (ed) Dublin: Dominican Publications Orbis Books

Smith, A (2000) *'New Age Spirituality' and A Christian Perspective.* In Spirituality Vol 6 November/December, Jordan, T (Ed)Dublin: Dominican Publications Orbis Books

Soelle, D (1984) *The Strength of the Weak: Toward a Christian Feminist Identity.* Philadelphia: The Westminster Press

Soelle, D (1992) *Celebrating Resistance: The Way of the Cross in Latin*

America. London: Mowbray

Soelle, D (2001) *The Silent Cry Mysticism and Resistance.* Minneapolis: Fortress Press

Steindl-Rast, D (1996) *The Spiritual Experience.* In God in All Worlds–An Anthology of Contemporary Spiritual Writing, Vardey, L (ed)New York: Vintage Books

Tauli-Corpuz, V (1996) *Reclaiming Earth-based Spirituality.* In Women Healing Earth–Third World Women on Ecology, Feminism and Religion, Ruether, R (ed) New York: Orbis Books

Templeton, J (1999) *Agape Love A Tradition Found in Eight World Religions.* London and Philadephia: Templeton Foundation Press

Tensin Gyatso, The Dali Lama (1999) *Ancient Wisdom, Modern World Ethics for a New Millennium.* London: Little, Brown and Company (UK)

Torbert, W (2000) *"Transforming Social Science: To Integrate Quantitative, Qualitative, and Action Research."* In Transforming Social Inquiry, Transforming Social Action: New Paradigms for Crossing the Theory/practice Divide in Universities and Communities Torbert and Sherman (eds) Kluwer Academic Publishers

Tosey, P *Inquiring into an Organisation's Energy: Applying a Education Perspective in Organisational Consultancy. Http://www.inspiring-change.co.uk/uk- more.htm* (Accessed 15 October 2001)

Underhill, E *Life as Prayer.* An Address given to a Fellowship of Prayer and issued by permission of the author (date not in the booklet) Edinburgh: United Free Church of Scotland, Publications Department

Underhill, E (1929) *The House of the Soul.* London: Methuen and Co, Ltd

Underhill, E (1995) *The Fruits of the Spirit.* Harrisburg, PA: Morehouse Publishing

Vardy, L (ed.) (1996) *God in All Worlds: An Anthology of Contemporary Spiritual Writing.* New York: Vintage Books

Vaughan, F (1995) *The Inward Arc: Healing in Psychotherapy and Spirituality.* Nevada: Blue Dolphin

Waddock, S (2000) *Linking Community and Spirit: A Commentary and Some Propositions.* Scranton: The University of Scranton Press

Webb, C (1994) *Feminist Research: Definitions Methodology, Methods and Evaluation.* In Research and Its Application Smith, J (ed) Oxford: Blackwell Scientific Publication

Wenger, E (1999) *Communities of Practice Learning, Meaning and Identity.* Cambridge: Cambridge University Press

West, W (2000) *Psychotherapy and Spirituality.* London: Sage Publications

West, W (2001) *Retreats: Time to Re-member Yourself. In Association for Pastoral* Care and Counselling Newsletter August, 2001, Marsh, J (ed) Rugby: APSCC

Wilber, K (1997) *A Spirituality that Transforms.* In What is Enlightenment Fall/Winter 1997 23-32

Williams, R (2002) *Soul Searching: The New Archbishop of Canterbury on the Mystic Who has Inspired Him.* The Times Cover Story 12 September 2002, page 2

Wilson Schaef, A (1999) *Living in Process: Basic Truths for Living the Path of the Soul.* New York: Ballentine Wellspring

Winter, M (2009) *Paradoxology: Spirituality in a Quantum Universe.* Maryknoll, New York: Orbis Books

World Summit for Sustainable Development (2001) *First meeting of the Secretary General's Advisory Panel 29 October. http://www. johannesburgsummit.org/html/basic_info/basicinfo.html)*

Worsley, R (2000) *"Can we talk about the Spirituality of Counselling?"* In Counselling, March 2000, Barden, N (ed) Rugby: Counselling – The Monthly Professional Journal for Counsellors, British Association for Counselling

Worsley, R (2000) *Affirming Spirituality* In Counselling, December

2000 Barden, N (ed) Rugby: Counselling–The Monthly Professional Journal for Counsellors, British Association for Counselling

Younge, G (2002) *Images that mock reality–beware bodies that use diversity not to promote fairness, but to make themselves appear fashionable.* In The Guardian, 5 August, p 15

Zappone, K (1991) *The Hope for Wholeness.* Connecticut: Twenty-Third Publications

Zohar, D and Marshall, I (2000) *SQ–Spiritual Intelligence: The Ultimate Intelligence.* London: Bloomsbury Publishing PLC

Zohar, D and Marshall, I (1994) *The Quantum Society: Mind, Physics, and a New Social Vision.* New York: Quill

Zohar, D (1991) *The Quantum Self.* London: Flamingo

Zuber-Skerrit, O (1994) *Professional Development in Higher Education: A Theoretical Framework for Action Research.* London: Kogan Page

Useful Websites

My idea here is to include relevant and helpful websites as well as the above bibliography so that people can continue to research, study and learn at their own pace according to their own interests. There is so much on the web today. Some of it, to my mind, is healthy and helpful and some is not.

Consciousness

Berkana–Art of Hosting: Ontario (http://berkana.org/berkana/index.php?option=com_content&task=category&sectionid=14&id=198&Itemid=322)

Brian Swimme on Pierre Teilhard de Chardin: The Divinization of the Cosmos (http://www.enlightennext.org/magazine/j19/teilhard.asp)

Center for Human Emergence (http://www.humanemergence

.org/)

DO Lectures | Tamsin Omond (http://www.dolectures.co.uk speakers/tamsin-omond)

Evolution of Spirituality—WIE.org (http://www.enlighten next.org/magazine/evolution-of-spirituality/)

Evolutionary Enlightenment Intensive with Andrew Cohen (http://www.andrewcohen.org/retreats/tuscany-09.asp? ecp=wc-072309#anc2)

GCI Movie *(http://www.glcoherence.org/index.php?option=com_con tent&task=view&id=60&sectionid=4)*

Global Coherence Initiative – (www.globalcoherence.org*)*

Open Space World Map (http://www.openspaceworldmap.org/)

Resurgence • Issue 251–Feasting and Fasting: Connecting the Plate and the Planet (http://www.resurgence.org/magazine/)

Science of Mind On Line (http://www.scienceofmind.com/)

The authentic self: a mysterious impulse to evolve –Andrewcohen.org (http://www.andrewcohen.org/teachings /authentic-self.asp)

Welcome to Caduceus Journal Magazine Online (http://www. caduceus.info/)

Welcome to The Great Rethinking: News (http://greatmy stery.org/)

What Is Enlightenment? – Redefining Spirituality for an Evolving World (http://www.enlightennext.org/magazine/)

YouTube–Joan Chittister: Science and Spirituality, Cortona, Italy 4 (http://www.youtube.com/watch?v=usVqpi_M5ec&feature =related)

Scientific American
https://dub116.mail.live.com/mail/#
news@email.scientificamerican.com

The Shift Network
https://dub116.mail.live.com/mail/#

Global Coherence Initiative
https://dub116.mail.live.com/mail/#

Spirituality and Health
*http://cl.s4.exct.net/?qs=d069e5ffa5cbab147b2f1399a9bac4ea678daac2b
bbeba1558227984cc093e83*
Barbara Marx Hubbard
https://dub116.mail.live.com/mail/#

Living School for Action and Contemplation
*http://r20.rs6.net/tn.jsp?e=001KpKLlA3SQrYUGnyowLP63ZsAlx1jr
mUPnBH6bYRSYmErxIISokYBt1fkQBCDnrTPogNPoLpPYRDPJ
O0cLMIslFsCDRdrpn_KhCU7G019qipA3p_f5o_BEw==*

Science and Nonduality

https://dub116.mail.live.com/mail/#

The Scientific and Medical Network - an interdisciplinary
networking forum and educational charity exploring science,
medicine, philosophy and spirituality. *www.scimednet.org*
Green Spirit
*http://r20.rs6.net/tn.jsp?e=001iDMqlxsPEy5W0l_UaJWyB_q7agsNV
bvTxuEzkkBT_R5wXVix8HjBfx2u3z71tWO2P4FOvktLy7p2RrVv
Z1EfnWAfQa00tdrqWc_ZG7aR20zJEto1VQaw==*

Resurgence

*https://dub116.mail.live.com/Handlers/ImageProxy.mvc?bicild=&cana
ry=kCnJlCKicLOE0gGFO0D%2f7e1AkWbC2bYwmTquOzzLn%2
bg%3d0&url=http%3a%2f%2fih.constantcontact.com%2ffs022%2
f1102092709619%2fimg%2f172.jpg*

Schumacher College *https://dub116.mail.live.com/Handlers/Image
Proxy.mvc?bicild=&canary=kCnJlCKicLOE0gGFO0D%2f7e1AkW
bC2bYwmTquOzzLn%2bg%3d0&url=http%3a%2f%2fwww.schu
machercollege.org.uk%2fimages%2f1177.jpg*

Brian Swimme – u-tube videos on the Cosmic Story and also
Thomas Berry on the Earth Story *http://s.ytimg.com/y
t/img/pixel-vfl3z5WfW.gif*

Wisdom University - Wisdom University is a graduate school dedicated to catalyzing personal and professional renewal within the context of granting academic degrees.*https://www. wisdomuniversity.org/index.htm*

Peter Russell – Spirit of Now
http://www.peterrussell.com/images/nav_images/Home_over.png

Dr Amit Goswami – videos by Dr Goswami on Quantum perspectives
https://www.google.ca/search?q=amit+goswami&hl=en&prmd=imvnsb o&source=univ&tbm=vid&tbo=u&sa=X&ei=pvkGUJ63D6jd6wHc nLncCA&ved=0CIIBEKsE&biw=1366&bih=516

Dr Amit Goswami – Centre for Quantum Activism
http://www.amitgoswami.org/

What the Bleep do We Know – video about understanding the Quantum world
http://www.whatthebleep.com/images/title2.gif

David Suzuki Foundation
http://www.davidsuzuki.org/

The Club of Budapest – Professor Dr Irvin Lazlo
http://www.clubofbudapest.org/index.php

Joyce Rupp – Home page
http://www.joycerupp.com/images/joyceheader60.png

Professor Heather Eaton – St Paul's University, Canada – 3 video presentations on Environment
http://www.google.ca/url?sa=t&rct=j&q=&esrc=s&source=web&cd=10 &sqi=2&ved=0CGcQtwIwCQ&url=http%3A%2F%2Fwww.youtu

*be.com%2Fwatch%3Fv%3DN-TsFzTejVs&ei=JP0GUMym
Namn6wHv8tXTCA&usg=AFQjCNFqk1XP0HHY0UWcizp5-
MKVFsfYZQ*

Thomas Berry and the Earth Community
http://www.thomasberry.org/

Diarmuid O'Murchu – author of many books on spirituality
http://www.diarmuid13.com

IONS – Institute of Noetic Sciences
http://noetic.org/

Danah Zohar – written many books on Quantum understanding
  - Link
http://dzohar.com/
http://www.bing.com/?FORM=Z9FD1

Circle Books

Circle is a symbol of infinity and unity. It's part of a growing list of imprints, including o-books.net and zero-books.net.

Circle Books aims to publish books in Christian spirituality that are fresh, accessible, and stimulating.

Our books are available in all good English language bookstores worldwide. If you can't find the book on the shelves, then ask your bookstore to order it for you, quoting the ISBN and title. Or, you can order online—all major online retail sites carry our titles.

To see our list of titles, please view www.Circle-Books.com, growing by 80 titles per year.

Authors can learn more about our proposal process by going to our website and clicking on Your Company > Submissions.

We define Christian spirituality as the relationship between the self and its sense of the transcendent or sacred, which issues in literary and artistic expression, community, social activism, and practices. A wide range of disciplines within the field of religious studies can be called upon, including history, narrative studies, philosophy, theology, sociology, and psychology. Interfaith in approach, Circle Books fosters creative dialogue with non-Christian traditions.

And tune into MySpiritRadio.com for our book review radio show, hosted by June-Elleni Laine, where you can listen to authors discussing their books.

MySpiritRadio